THE WARRIOR AND THE SAGE

ENDLESS JOURNEY

MARK LOUDERMILK

PHOENIX & SAGE
PUBLISHING

PHOENIX & SAGE PUBLISHING

First Edition

ISBN: 979-8-9987658-2-7

Self-published by Mark Loudermilk

Cover design by Phoenix & Sage Publishing

This book is designed to provide accurate and authoritative information on the topics covered. It is sold with the understanding that neither the author nor the publisher is engaged in rendering legal, accounting, or other professional services. If expert assistance is required, the services of a competent professional should be sought.

The stories, experiences, and examples shared in this book are based on the author's real-life experiences and observations. Some names and identifying details have been changed to protect the privacy of individuals.

Success in business, as in life, is the result of preparation, hard work,learning from failure, loyalty, and persistence. This book provides guidance,but results will vary based on numerous factors specific to your situation.

To all those on the path of self-discovery— may you find the courage of a warrior and the wisdom of a sage on your endless journey.

"The greatest journey you will ever take is the one from your head to your heart, from who you think you are to who you truly are."

"We are not human beings having a spiritual experience. We are spiritual beings having a human experience." — Pierre Teilhard de Chardin

PREFACE

When I set out to write this book, I had one simple goal: to create the guide I wish I'd had during my own darkest moments of confusion and struggle.

The path of personal growth isn't easy. It's filled with challenges,setbacks, and moments of doubt. Yet it remains the most worthwhile journey we can undertake—the journey to become who we truly are.

I've gathered wisdom from ancient philosophy, modern psychology, and my own experiences to create both a map for your journey and a toolkit to help you navigate the terrain. Some of these lessons I learned the hard way, through painful mistakes and hard-won insights. Others came through studying the lives and teachings of those who walked this path before us.

This book doesn't promise overnight transformation or magic solutions.Instead, it offers something more valuable: a practical framework for sustainable growth and authentic living. The integration of timeless principles with daily practices creates a path that anyone can follow, one step at a time.

Whether you're at the beginning of your personal development journey or well along the path, my hope is that these pages serve as both compass and companion as you discover your own unique expression of the warrior's courage and the sage's wisdom.

The journey is endless, but that is its beauty. There is always another horizon, another level of growth to explore. And in that continuous unfolding lies the joy of becoming.

May you find something in these pages that lights your way.

With gratitude,

Mark Loudermilk

INTRODUCTION

The Path Begins

Welcome to a journey of personal transformation. In the pages that follow, you'll discover powerful principles and practices that can help you become the person you aspire to be—someone who lives with purpose, clarity, and fulfillment.

The path we'll walk together combines ancient wisdom with modern insights, philosophical depth with practical application. This isn't just a book to be read; it's an experience to be lived, a journey to be traveled step by reflective step.

The Journey Map

This book is organized as a natural progression, with each chapter building on the insights and skills of the previous one:

Chapter 1: Know Yourself — The Power of Honest Reflection

We begin with self-awareness—the courage to see yourself as you truly are, without illusion or excuse. This honest reflection forms the foundation for all other growth.

Chapter 2: Building Your Compass — Choosing the Principles That Guide You

Once you see yourself clearly, you'll define the values and principles that will guide your decisions and actions. This inner compass provides direction and stability in an ever-changing world.

Chapter 3: Brick by Brick — The Power of Daily Discipline

With your compass established, you'll develop the discipline to align your daily actions with your deepest values, building consistency that transforms intentions into reality.

Chapter 4: Mastering the Inner Game — Mind and Emotions

Here we explore how to work with your thoughts and emotions rather than being controlled by them, cultivating a mindset that supports your growth rather than sabotages it.

Chapter 5: Physical Well-Being and Energy — Strengthening Your Foundation

Your physical body is the vehicle for your journey. This chapter addresses how physical well-being enhances every other aspect of personal development.

Chapter 6: The Power of Connection

No meaningful journey happens in isolation. We examine how to build and nurture relationships that support your growth while contributing to others' well-being.

Chapter 7: Purpose and Direction — Designing Your Life

With the essential tools in place, you'll learn to design a life of meaning and purpose, setting a course that reflects your authentic self and deepest aspirations.

Chapter 8: Conclusion and Next Steps — Embodying Your New Identity

Finally, we integrate all you've learned into a sustainable path forward, with practical guidance for continuing your journey of growth.

The Book and Toolkit: Theory Meets Practice

What makes this approach unique is the integration of philosophical understanding with practical application. Throughout the book, you'll find two complementary components:

The Main Chapters provide the context, principles, and stories that help you understand *why* certain practices matter and how they work to transform your life. These chapters offer the theoretical foundation and inspiration.

The Practical Toolkit contains specific exercises, techniques, and practices that show you *how*to apply these principles in your daily life. The toolkit transforms abstract concepts into concrete action steps.

To help you navigate between these components, you'll find **Toolkit References** throughout each chapter that direct you to relevant practices:

TOOLKIT REFERENCE

To apply these principles about self-awareness, see "The Honest Mirror Exercise" and "Thought Patterns Tracking" in Section 1 of thePractical Toolkit.

Think of the main chapters as providing the map for your journey, while the toolkit offers the specific vehicles and tools you'll need along the way.

How to Use This Book

There are several ways to approach this material, depending on your needs and learning style:

The Sequential Journey: Read each chapter from beginning to end, pausing to practice the corresponding toolkit exercises before moving to the next chapter. This provides a structured, comprehensive approach to building your personal growth foundation.

The Targeted Approach: If you're facing a specific challenge, you might jump to the relevant chapter (e.g., "Mastering the Inner Game" for emotional struggles)and its corresponding toolkit section. Each chapter can stand alone, though they're most powerful when understood as part of the whole.

The Immersive Experience: Some readers prefer to read the entire book first to grasp the big picture, then return to the beginning and work through each chapter with its toolkit practices. This gives you both context and application.

The Ongoing Resource: After your first journey through the material, keep the book accessible as a reference. When facing a decision or challenge, return to relevant chapters and toolkit sections for guidance and renewed perspective.

Whichever approach you choose, I encourage you to engage deeply with both the principles and the practices. Knowledge without application remains theoretical; practice without understanding lacks direction. Together, they create transformation.

A Note on the Journey

Personal growth isn't about reaching a perfect destination. It's about moving in a meaningful direction, one step at a time. There will be moments of insight and breakthrough, and there will be times of struggle and setback. Both are part of the path.

Be patient with yourself. Celebrate progress, not perfection. Each small choice to grow compounds over time into remarkable change. The journey may be endless, but that is its beauty—there is always another level of wisdom to embody, another aspect of potential to realize.

As the ancient Chinese proverb says: "The journey of a thousand miles begins with a single step." This book is an invitation to take that step, and then another, and another—with courage, compassion, and commitment.

Let's begin.

CONTENTS

1

———— ◦ ————

KNOW YOURSELF — THE POWER OF HONEST REFLECTION

"The path to wisdom begins with the courage to see yourself as you truly are."

The Mirror Moment

Marcus stood in the bathroom, hands braced against the cool marble of the sink, staring into his own reflection in the dim evening light. The silence of his apartment enveloped him, broken only by the steady drip of the faucet and the distant hum of city traffic below. He looked into his own eyes—those familiar yet somehow foreign eyes—searching for something he couldn't name.

Just hours ago, another project at work had collapsed. The client rejected the proposal his team had spent weeks preparing. His boss's disappointment had been palpable during their tense phone call, and the argument with Sophia afterward—his third in as many weeks with his girlfriend—had left him feeling hollow and defensive. As he stood there, the weight of these failures pressed down on his shoulders like an invisible burden.

Nothing ever works out for me, he thought bitterly. *No matter how hard I try.*

In that moment of solitude, Marcus felt the overwhelming urge to turn away from the mirror, to reach for his phone and lose himself in the comfortable numbness of mindless scrolling. Facing himself—truly *seeing* himself—was the one thing he'd been skillfully avoiding for years.

Yet something kept him rooted there, eyes locked on his reflection. It was as if a quiet voice from within whispered, *"Stay."* His heart pounded as if sensing danger. What was he afraid of seeing if he truly looked? What truths lurked beneath the surface of his carefully constructed explanations and excuses?

A quote he had once heard floated into his consciousness: **"The truth will set you free, but first it will make you uncomfortable."** Marcus couldn't remember where he'd encountered those words, but they pierced through his defenses with unexpected clarity.

Deep down, beneath layers of justification and self-protection, he recognized that all his life, he had been running—running from the one conversation he needed most desperately to have: the honest conversation with himself. And somewhere in his heart, he suspected that this quiet confrontation in the mirror might be the only path out of the recurring cycles of his life.

TOOLKIT REFERENCE *To begin your own mirror moment practice, see "The Honest Reflection Exercise" and "Discomfort Tolerance Technique" in Section 1 of the Practical Toolkit.*

The Pattern Becomes Visible

As Marcus continued to hold his own gaze, memories began to surface—not randomly, but in a pattern he had never before allowed himself to see.

He saw himself storming out of his previous workplace, blaming his "micromanaging" boss for the project failures that had actually stemmed from his own procrastination and half-finished efforts. He recalled the hurt in Sophia's eyes last month when she'd said, "You never really listen to me," and how quickly he'd dismissed her concern as an over-reaction. He remembered the friendship with David that had disintegrated after a heated argument—an argument in which Marcus had convinced himself he was completely in the right.

In every memory, in every disappointment and conflict, Marcus had crafted a narrative that placed the blame squarely outside himself. Bad management. Unreasonable expectations. Other people's shortcomings. Unfortunate timing. That had been the story of his life: *It's not my fault.*

But tonight, standing unflinching before his own reflection, another possibility emerged—a harder, more uncomfortable truth: What if the common denominator in all these situations was... him?

The thought landed like a stone in still water, sending ripples of recognition through his consciousness. It wasn't that Marcus was uniquely flawed or terrible—it was that he had never truly looked at his own role in his life's challenges. He had been, as philosopher Carl Jung might say, projecting his shadows onto the external world.

Jung's words seemed to speak directly to him in this moment: *"Until you make the unconscious conscious, it will direct your life and you will call it fate."* Marcus had stumbled through years feeling that fate or luck was against him, never realizing he himself might be unconsciously repeating patterns that created similar outcomes again and again.

His chest tightened as the weight of this realization settled upon him. He splashed cold water on his face, the shock of it like an awakening—bracing and necessary. Drying his face with a towel, Marcus recognized he stood at a profound crossroads. One path was familiar and comfortable: turn away from the mirror, go to bed nursing his grievances, and continue tomorrow as he always had—blaming others, deflecting responsibility, remaining trapped in cycles of frustration and disappointment.

The other path was unknown, difficult, and beckoned with both promise and challenge: to finally hold himself accountable, to own his part in his struggles, no matter how uncomfortable it might be to admit.

In that raw, unguarded moment, Marcus made a decision. He would try, at least for a little while, to see himself with unflinching honesty. He would examine his own behavior without the protective filter of excuses and self-justification.

"The door to transformation opens from the inside," he thought to himself, the words emerging from some deeper wisdom he hadn't known he possessed. If he wanted his life to change, he had to find the courage to see who he truly was today, with all his strengths and flaws laid bare.

TOOLKIT REFERENCE *To identify your own recurring patterns, explore the "Life Pattern Recognition" and "Common Denominator Analysis" in Section 1 of the Practical Toolkit.*

The Accountability Journey Begins

The next morning, with resolve still fresh in his mind, Marcus reached out to someone he hadn't spoken to in months: Richard, a former manager who had always given him straight, unvarnished feedback. They met at a quiet café tucked away from the bustle of downtown.

As steam rose from his coffee cup, Marcus found himself pouring out his frustrations—the difficult boss, the colleagues who didn't pull their weight, the relationship troubles, the never-ending string of setbacks. Richard listened attentively, his expression neither judgmental nor particularly sympathetic, simply present and engaged.

When Marcus finally ran out of words, Richard reached into his messenger bag and pulled out a simple, leather-bound notebook. He slid it across the table.

"Marcus," he said, his voice gentle but firm, "I'd like you to try something for me. For one week—just seven days—I want you to write down what happens each day. But here's the real challenge: every time something goes wrong or you feel let down, I want you to ask yourself a question."

"What question?" Marcus asked, already feeling a twinge of defensiveness.

"What was *my* part in this?" Richard said. "And then write that down too."

Marcus shook his head, a familiar frustration rising. "My part? Honestly, I don't think I *had* a part in most of what's happening. That project failed because Tom dropped the ball completely—he missed the deadline for his section, and the whole thing fell apart."

Richard held up a hand. "I'm not saying everything is your fault," he clarified. "I'm saying just *look* for your part. Even if it's only 5% of the situation, own that 5%. This journal is only for your eyes—no one else will see it. So be brutally honest. No excuses, no blaming—just truth." He tapped the notebook. "Can you do that? For just one week?"

Marcus stared at the blank notebook, its empty pages both inviting and somehow threatening. The request made him deeply uncomfortable—which, he realized with a start, might be precisely why he needed to do it. He thought of his moment at the mirror the night before, the commitment he'd made to himself.

"Alright," he agreed, taking the notebook. "One week."

That evening, Marcus sat at his kitchen table, the blank page before him somehow more intimidating than any work presentation he'd ever faced. He wrote the date at the top, then began to recount the day's events. His pen moved easily at first, describing meetings and conversations.

But when he reached the part about a minor disagreement with a coworker over project timelines, he paused. His instinct was to write about how unreasonable the coworker had been, how they didn't understand the complexity of Marcus's portion of the work. But then he remembered: *What was my part?*

His jaw tightened. After a long moment, he forced himself to write: "I didn't communicate clearly about how long my section would take. I knew last week I'd need more time but didn't say anything because I didn't want to look inefficient."

The words stared back at him from the page, stark and uncomfortably true. Something shifted in him—a small release, as if a tightly wound spring had loosened just one turn. It wasn't pleasant exactly, but there was an odd relief in the admission.

He continued through the day's events, including a brief exchange with Sophia that had ended with her sighing in frustration. Again, he forced himself to look for his part: "I was only half-listening while she talked about her day because I was checking email on my phone. I probably missed something important to her."

With each admission, the process became simultaneously more difficult and liberating. It was as if he were lancing small wounds—painful in the moment, but ultimately releasing pressure that had been building beneath the surface.

TOOLKIT REFERENCE *To develop your personal accountability practice, see "The Ownership Journal" and "The 5% Rule" exercises in Section 1 of the Practical Toolkit.*

Uncovering the Truth Within

Over the next days, Marcus continued his journaling practice with growing insight. Some entries were brief; others stretched for pages as he wrestled with harder truths about himself. He began to notice patterns in his behavior that had been invisible to him before:

When projects grew challenging at work, he often disengaged, putting in minimal effort while crafting ready excuses for why things weren't progressing. When disagreements arose in his relationship, he frequently shut down emotionally, making Sophia feel unheard and eventually provoking the very arguments he claimed to want to avoid.

On Wednesday evening, Marcus found himself actually looking forward to his journaling time—not because it was easy, but because each honest admission felt like removing a small stone from a bag he'd been carrying for years. The weight he bore was lightening, one truth at a time.

On Friday, reviewing his week's entries, a profound realization struck him: **"We don't see things as they are; we see them as *we* are."** The thought came to him with such clarity that he wrote it down in bold letters at the bottom of the page. His perception of events had been colored—even distorted—by his own fears, defenses, and blind spots. How much of what he had seen as bad luck or others' failings was actually the natural consequence of his own choices and attitudes?

This wasn't about self-flagellation or dwelling in guilt. Rather, for the first time, Marcus felt a strange sense of power emerging through his honesty. If he had been creating some of his own problems, then he also had the power to create different outcomes. The victim narrative that had defined so many of his internal stories began to crumble, replaced by something far more empowering: agency and choice.

"True freedom begins with taking responsibility for the one life you can control—your own," he wrote in his journal. The insight didn't come from any book or mentor; it emerged from his own deepening self-awareness.

By Sunday evening, as Marcus reviewed his week of reflections, he felt simultaneously humbled and strengthened. The experience had been uncomfortable, yes—at times deeply so. But it had also been illuminating in ways he hadn't anticipated. He had begun to see himself more clearly, without the filters of self-justification that had clouded his vision for so long.

There was a strange lightness in this new clarity. Marcus wasn't naive enough to think that one week of honest journaling had solved all his problems. But he had taken the first crucial step on a path toward genuine change: seeing himself as he truly was, not as he wished to appear.

TOOLKIT REFERENCE*For deeper self-awareness practices, explore "The Truth-Seeking Questions" and "Defense Mechanism Identification" in Section 1 of the Practical Toolkit.*

From Awareness to Action

The real test of Marcus's emerging self-awareness came the following week, when he returned to the same challenges with new eyes.

On Monday morning, his team met to regroup after the failed proposal. His boss outlined what had gone wrong and asked for suggestions on how to recover with the client. In the past, Marcus would have subtly directed blame toward colleagues or circumstances. This time, something different happened.

"I think I contributed to the problem," he said, surprising even himself with the words. "I didn't speak up about some concerns I had with our approach because I didn't want to seem negative. And I could have reached out to the client more during the process to make sure we were aligned." The words came out steadily, without the usual defensive edge.

A brief silence followed. His boss looked at him with what might have been respect. "Thank you for that, Marcus. That's helpful perspective." The meeting continued with a more collaborative tone than usual.

Later that day, when Sophia texted about dinner plans, Marcus caught himself about to send a noncommittal response while in the middle of a task. Instead, remembering his journal insights about not being present with her, he set his work aside for a moment and called her instead of texting.

"Hey, I wanted to actually talk instead of just texting," he told her. "And I wanted to properly apologize for last week. You were trying to tell me something important, and I wasn't really listening."

The surprise and warmth in her voice was immediate. "Thank you for saying that," she said. "That means a lot to me."

Neither of these moments was dramatic or earth-shattering. They didn't instantly solve all the challenges in Marcus's work or relationship. But they represented something significant: the gap between awareness and action was beginning to close. Marcus wasn't just seeing his patterns; he was starting to change them.

Over the weeks that followed, this trend continued. With each small choice to respond differently—to take responsibility rather than deflect it, to listen deeply rather than defend himself, to engage fully rather than withdraw—Marcus felt a growing sense of congruence between the person he wanted to be and the person he was becoming.

"Every time you choose truth over comfort, you build integrity," he wrote in his journal one evening. **"And integrity is the foundation that everything else stands on."**

There were still difficult days, of course. Old habits of defensiveness and blame would resurface, especially when he felt stressed or threatened. But now Marcus could recognize these patterns more quickly. The time between falling into an old behavior and becoming aware of it grew shorter. Eventually, he could often catch himself in the moment, just before he would have defaulted to a familiar but unhelpful response.

This, Marcus realized, was the true power of honest self-reflection: it created a space between stimulus and response, a space in which he could choose differently. And with each choice, he was essentially rewiring his brain, creating new neural pathways that made better responses more automatic over time.

TOOLKIT REFERENCE *To bridge awareness and action in your own life, practice "The Response Gap Technique" and "Pattern Interruption" in Section 1 of the Practical Toolkit.*

The Ongoing Journey of Self-Discovery

Three months after his first night of honest self-reflection, Marcus met Richard again at the same café. The worn leather journal sat between them, now filled with daily entries, insights, and moments of both struggle and breakthrough.

"So," Richard asked, stirring his coffee, "what have you learned?"

Marcus considered the question carefully. "I've learned that I was telling myself stories that kept me stuck," he began. "Stories about how things 'happened to me' rather than acknowledging the choices I was making. I've learned that it's easier to blame others than to look at myself, but it's also less effective."

He tapped the journal. "Most importantly, I've learned that self-honesty isn't a one-time event. It's a practice—something I have to recommit to every day."

Richard nodded. "That's wisdom worth having."

"There's something else," Marcus added after a moment. "I used to think that looking too closely at my flaws would make me feel terrible about myself. But it's had the opposite effect. There's a kind of... freedom in not having to maintain the illusion of perfection. I can just be human—flawed, learning, growing. And that feels more authentic than any image I was trying to project before."

"True confidence comes not from believing you're flawless, but from knowing you can face your flaws with courage," Richard said. "That's what I've always seen in you, Marcus—not the perfection you were trying to project, but the potential to be authentic."

As they parted ways, Marcus realized something profound had shifted in him over these months. He was beginning to trust himself—not to be perfect, but to be honest. To look at reality as it was, not as he wished it to be. To own his part in his life's challenges and, in doing so, to claim his power to create change.

The journey of self-knowledge wasn't complete—it never would be. There would always be new layers to uncover, new blind spots to illuminate, new patterns to recognize. But Marcus had taken the essential first step: he had decided to walk the path of truth rather than comfort.

And on that path, he had discovered that the person he was capable of becoming was far more compelling than the illusion he had been trying to maintain.

TOOLKIT REFERENCE *To sustain your self-awareness practice, explore "The Continuous Growth Mindset" and "Truth-Seeking Habits" in Section 1 of the Practical Toolkit.*

A Personal Note: My Own Mirror Moment

I still remember my own mirror moment with stark clarity—not a physical mirror, but a question that reflected my soul back to me with unforgiving honesty.

In my late twenties, I had mastered the art of external achievement while remaining internally hollow. On paper, my life looked impressive—financial success, academic credentials, the trappings of what society labels "making it." Yet beneath this carefully constructed facade, I was repeating destructive patterns with alarming consistency. Relationships crumbled around me. My psychological landscape had darkened into what psychologists might diplomatically call "dark triad" tendencies—a toxic blend of narcissism, manipulation, Machiavellian and psychopathy forged from growing up in a world of gangs, killers and prison inmates.

The most insidious part? I had convinced myself that everyone else was the problem. My relationships failed because others weren't committed enough. My emotional turbulence existed because the world was unfair. I had perfected the art of externalizing blame while remaining blind to my own contribution to my suffering.

Then came the moment that cracked the foundation of my self-deception. It arrived not in some dramatic crisis, but in the gentle voice of my mother during an ordinary phone call. As I rambled through my usual litany of complaints about others, she interrupted with four simple words: "Are you happy, Mark?"

The question struck me like a physical blow. Time seemed to freeze. In that suspended moment, the elaborate architecture of excuses I had built began to crumble. I stammered an automatic "Of course I am," but the words rang hollow even as they left my lips.

That question became a splinter in my mind that I couldn't remove. It followed me through meetings, into relationships, and kept me awake at night. "Are you happy?" Four words that demanded what I had been avoiding for years—honest self-reflection.

"The most painful truth will set you free faster than the most comforting lie will keep you safe."

When I finally gathered the courage to sit with this question—to really examine myself without the shield of self-deception—what I saw was humbling. I had wandered so far from my authentic self that the person staring back from the metaphorical mirror was nearly unrecognizable. The values I claimed to hold stood in stark contrast to how I was actually living. The blame I cast outward was merely a shadow of the responsibility I had refused to accept.

This is the paradox of honest reflection: it is both the most terrible and the most beautiful moment in personal growth. Terrible because we must face our own shadow without flinching; beautiful because only then can genuine transformation begin. As one ancient sage put it, "The cave you fear to enter holds the treasure you seek."

Like Marcus in our story, I began keeping a journal. Each evening, I documented moments of self-deception, patterns of blame, instances where my actions contradicted my proclaimed values. At first, each entry felt like pressing on a bruise. But gradually, something shifted. The very act of acknowledging these patterns began to loosen their grip on me.

"Self-awareness is the first glimmer of dawn after a night of unconscious living."

This experience taught me something profound: honest self-reflection isn't merely a philosophical exercise or a self-help technique—it's the foundation of an authentic life.

Without the courage to see ourselves clearly, we remain prisoners of our own making, captives to patterns we don't even recognize.

I share this not because my story is remarkable, but because I believe we all face these pivotal moments where truth extends an invitation toward a more authentic path. The question is not whether this invitation will come, but whether we will have the courage to accept it when it arrives.

For me, it came in the form of my mother's question. For you, it might appear differently—perhaps through a relationship that ends, a career setback, or simply a persistent feeling that something essential is missing. The form matters less than our response.

"The moment you embrace the truth you've been avoiding is the moment your future self begins to thank you."

The journey of self-discovery is rarely comfortable, but it is infinitely rewarding. When we find the courage to look in the mirror without flinching—to see ourselves as we truly are rather than as we wish to be seen—we take the first step toward authentic transformation. Because without identifying who we truly are, how could we ever hope to become who we're meant to be?

What mirror moment awaits you? And when it comes, will you have the courage to look?

Becoming Your Own Explorer

Marcus's story and my own might resonate with you. In our own ways, we all wear comfortable blinders that shield us from uncomfortable truths. We tell ourselves little lies that help us avoid guilt or pain: *"It's not my fault... I did my best... I'll change soon... Others have it easier."* These stories we weave can lull us into stagnation. But when we dare to remove those blinders, we start seeing the patterns in our lives with crystal clarity. And with clarity comes the ability to chart a new course.

How can **you** begin this journey of self-exploration? You don't need a dramatic crisis or a mentor to hand you a journal (though life has a funny way of providing both when needed). You can start right here, right now, by becoming an explorer of your own inner world. Pretend for a moment that *you* are both the scientist and the subject of an important study. Your job is to observe yourself—gently, without judgment—and map out the territory of *you*.

"The most challenging expedition you'll ever undertake is the journey into your own heart and mind," but it's also the most rewarding. This exploration requires courage, compassion, and curiosity—three qualities that will serve you well throughout your personal growth journey.

Self-Exploration Questions

Take a moment now to consider these questions. You might want to write down your answers in a journal or notebook:

1. **Emotional Patterns:** When was the last time you felt intensely angry, anxious, or hurt? What specifically triggered this emotion? Does this trigger show up repeatedly in your life?

2. **Habitual Responses:** When you feel criticized, do you typically: defend yourself immediately, withdraw emotionally, counter-attack, or seek to understand the feedback? What does this pattern reveal about your deeper beliefs?

3. **Self-Talk Awareness:** What phrases do you repeatedly tell yourself? Complete this sentence with your first thought: "Deep down, I believe I am..."

4. **Personal Responsibility:** In your most challenging relationship right now, what is your contribution to the difficulty? (Remember, this doesn't mean taking all the blame, just honestly assessing your part.)

5. **Values Check:** When have you felt most proud of yourself recently? What value or principle were you honoring in that moment?

Start with your emotions. Pay attention the next time you feel a surge of anger, a stab of anxiety, or a wave of sadness. Instead of brushing it aside, pause and curiously examine it. What triggered it? Did a colleague's offhand comment send you spiraling? Did seeing a photo on social media make your chest tighten with envy or loneliness? Note these moments down, maybe in a phone app or a pocket notebook.

Over a week or two, patterns will emerge like constellations in the night sky. Perhaps you'll discover, *"I get anxious every Sunday night as the work week looms"* or *"Every time I feel ignored, I become angry and snappish."* These emotional patterns are golden clues, each pointing to deeper beliefs or wounds. Maybe that anger at feeling ignored hints at a belief that "I'm not respected," or that Sunday anxiety whispers "I'm not prepared enough for what's coming." When you spot a constellation of emotion, you begin to understand the shape of your inner landscape.

Next, observe your habits and behaviors, especially the ones on autopilot. We are all creatures of habit—our days often follow a rhythm set by routines we've repeated for years. Take a step back and watch yourself as if you were in a documentary. In the morning, do you snooze your alarm multiple times and then rush frantically (setting a tone of stress for the day)? When you're faced with a difficult task, do you find yourself opening new browser tabs or apps, seeking distraction? What do you reach for when you're tired or down—a bag of chips, a cigarette, the phone to call a friend and vent?

There's no need to immediately change any of it; for now, just notice and note it down. As Marcus learned, **"You can't change a habit you don't even realize you have."** So shine a gentle light on these routines. You might realize, for example, "I stay up past midnight scrolling through my phone most nights, and I'm exhausted every morning." That's a pattern. Or "Every time I have a free weekend, I somehow end up volunteering for extra work because I can't say no." That's a pattern, too. Each one you identify is like discovering a piece of a puzzle. Put the pieces together, and you get a picture of how you operate day-to-day.

Common Self-Talk Patterns

Now, perhaps the most subtle observation: your self-talk—the quiet, constant monologue of thoughts about yourself. This inner voice can be a trickster. It often plays old recordings we've internalized over years. Here are some common patterns to watch for:

The Perfectionist: "I should have done better. This isn't good enough. I can't rest until it's flawless."

The Impostor: "I don't really deserve this. Soon everyone will figure out I don't know what I'm doing."

The Catastrophizer: "This will be a disaster. Everything's going to fall apart. I'll never recover from this."

The Comparer: "Everyone else has it together. Look how successful/happy/confident they are compared to me."

The Harsh Judge: "I'm so stupid/lazy/worthless. Why can't I just get it right for once?"

Listen to the tone you use with yourself. Do you encourage yourself, or do you harshly criticize every misstep? When someone compliments you, does that voice accept it graciously or immediately dismiss it, saying, "They're just being polite"?

When you make a mistake, do you think, "Ah, I *always* do that, I'm hopeless,"? These spontaneous thoughts reveal the beliefs you hold about your worth and abilities.

Write them down when you catch them. Bringing these hidden beliefs into the light is huge—because once you see them, you can ask, "Wait, is this actually true?" Often, you'll find it's not; it's just a story you've been carrying, perhaps since childhood, that *feels* true. But feelings aren't facts, and seeing the story is the first step to rewriting it.

"Your most important conversations are the ones you have with yourself," because they shape how you interpret and respond to everything else. Make sure those conversations are based in truth and compassion, not distortion and judgment.

TOOLKIT REFERENCE *To begin your self-exploration journey, see "The Three-Domain Awareness Practice" and "Self-Talk Monitoring" in Section 1 of the Practical Toolkit.*

The Courage to Be Honest

As you gather these observations about your feelings, habits, and self-talk, remember to do it with compassion. You are not building this self-portrait to beat yourself up or to label yourself as "a mess." You are diagnosing, not condemning. Think of yourself as that neutral scientist: curious, open-minded, determined to find the truth, but not here to judge or punish.

Yes, some of the truths you uncover will make you squirm—that's normal. It's okay to feel uncomfortable; in fact, it's a sign of progress. But try not to spiral into self-criticism. Instead, view each discovery as simply more data, valuable information about **where you are right now**. You might even imagine you're mapping out a starting point on a big journey. No matter how rugged the terrain appears (bad habits, emotional baggage and all), it's your current location—and acknowledging it fully means you're ready to navigate forward with accuracy.

Many people find it helpful to physically record these insights, just as Marcus did. Consider keeping a small journal or a notes app at hand for the next week or so, expressly for this purpose. Jot down the flash of irritation you felt in the afternoon meeting and what sparked it. Jot down the fact that you skipped lunch and then noticed yourself feeling very negative by evening (perhaps low blood sugar feeding anxious thoughts?). Write the kind comment your friend said that you had trouble believing. Treat it like gathering clues about yourself.

Over days, you will accumulate a precious record of *you*. Those notes will serve as a mirror just like Marcus's notebook did—reflecting back your triggers, your behaviors, and your beliefs. This self-awareness is incredibly empowering. In knowledge there is power: when you know that, say, **criticism from others** is a trigger that makes you feel small and react defensively, you can work on strengthening your confidence or reframing feedback so it doesn't wound you so deeply. When you know that **boredom leads you to procrastinate**, you can devise ways to make tasks more engaging or set up external accountability. But none of that change can happen until you first *see* the pattern clearly.

"Truth may be momentarily painful, but it is eventually liberating," unlike comfortable illusions, which feel good initially but trap you in the same patterns indefinitely. This is why honest self-reflection, though sometimes challenging, is ultimately the kindest thing you can do for yourself.

Through this process, you may experience moments of discomfort. In fact, you surely will. You might fill a few pages with examples of, say, how often you lie to yourself each day—even tiny lies like "just one more cookie" when you're not truly hungry, or "I'll start working in 5 minutes" which becomes 30. And when you look at those pages, a wave of discouragement might hit: *Is this really me? How did I not notice I do this all the time?*

It might feel like peering into that dusty attic of your mind, confronted with old, ugly furniture and cobwebs of past mistakes you'd rather not see. In those moments, remember that this is the very heart of growth. **"No butterfly emerges without first dissolving its old form in the chrysalis."** No meaningful transformation happens without the courage to see what needs to change.

When you feel the sting of regret or embarrassment, take a breath and silently acknowledge, *"This is the feeling of progress. It's uncomfortable, but I am growing."* Every courageous act of self-honesty, no matter how small, rewards you with a little more self-awareness, a little more strength. It's like lifting weights: the strain today builds the muscle you'll flex tomorrow.

There will be times you'll want to turn away—when the mirror shows an aspect of yourself you don't like. Perhaps you realize you've been careless with a loved one's feelings, or you haven't been as responsible as you believed. The instinct might be to shut the journal, to distract yourself, to say "Enough for today." And indeed, pace yourself—no one says you have to face every truth all at once to the point of overwhelm. But do gently challenge yourself to stay with the process.

When your mind offers excuses or says "This is silly, I don't need to do this," recognize that as resistance. Resistance often shows up right at the doorstep of meaningful change, trying to keep you in the comfort zone. Push past that door. Keep looking in that metaphorical mirror a little longer. **"Because once you see a truth, you can act on it—but if you never see it, it will quietly control you forever."**

Think again of Marcus. That week of honest reflection was not easy for him. It was humbling and at times emotional. But by its end, he felt a shift in his very identity. He went from feeling like a passive character in his life's story to feeling like the author. The same can be true for you. Every insight you gain is like reclaiming a piece of your power that you had unknowingly given away.

Figure 1: The cycle of self-awareness, showing how honest reflection leads to insight, which enables conscious choice, resulting in meaningful change and renewed awareness.

TOOLKIT REFERENCE *To build courage for honest self-reflection, try the "Discomfort Tolerance" and "Self-Compassion During Insight" practices in Section 1 of the Practical Toolkit.*

The Path Forward: From Insight to Transformation

Knowledge without action is merely information—potentially interesting, but ultimately ineffective at creating change. The goal of self-awareness isn't simply to accumulate insights about yourself; it's to use those insights to transform how you live.

"Understanding is the bridge between awareness and change," but you still have to cross that bridge. Once you've begun to see your patterns clearly, the natural next step is to ask: What will I do differently now?

This doesn't mean overhauling your entire life overnight. Start small. If you've realized you tend to interrupt others in conversation (a common insight people discover when they start paying attention), your action might be as simple as: "Today, I'll consciously pause and count to three before responding when someone else is speaking." If you've noticed you procrastinate on important tasks by checking email, your action might be: "I'll set a timer for 25 minutes of focused work before I allow myself to check messages."

These small changes, consistently applied, create ripples that expand outward into every area of your life. Just as Marcus found that his newfound honesty about his role in problems led to improved work relationships and a stronger connection with Sophia, your increasing self-awareness will naturally translate into better decisions, healthier boundaries, and more authentic relationships.

Remember that transformation is a process, not an event. You won't suddenly become a completely different person after a week of journaling or self-reflection. The path is more like a spiral than a straight line—you'll revisit similar themes and challenges at different levels of understanding. But with each return, you'll bring greater awareness and skill to the situation.

"Growth happens in spirals, not straight lines. You may pass the same point multiple times, but always at a different level." This is why patience and persistence are essential companions on the journey of self-discovery. Trust the process, even when progress seems slow or uneven.

As you continue to explore your inner landscape, maintain that balance of courage and compassion we discussed earlier. Be brave enough to face difficult truths about yourself, but kind enough to recognize that making mistakes and having blind spots is part of being human. We all have patterns we're working to change. The fact that you're engaged in this process at all puts you ahead of many who never muster the courage to look within.

"The most courageous act is not climbing mountains or facing external dangers—it is facing yourself with honesty and compassion." That journey inward requires more bravery than many outward adventures, but its rewards are immeasurable: authentic relationships, aligned purpose, inner peace, and the deep satisfaction of living consciously rather than reactively.

Journal Prompts for Self-Awareness

Take a few moments to reflect on these questions in writing:

1. What patterns in my life keep repeating that I'm tired of experiencing?

2. If I were completely honest with myself, what am I avoiding looking at?

3. What story do I tell myself about who I am? Is this story limiting me in any way?

4. When do I feel most authentically myself? What conditions or relationships bring out my best?

5. What one small change could I make today that would align my actions more closely with my values?

This first chapter in your personal development journey—the practice of honest self-reflection—is the foundation upon which everything else will be built.

2

— · —

BUILDING YOUR COMPASS — CHOOSING THE PRINCIPLES THAT GUIDE YOU

Imagine a lone ship at sea on a moonless night. The waters of life are choppy and the winds change without warning. Without a compass or a North Star, that ship would drift aimlessly, vulnerable to every gust. In much the same way, **we** drift in life if we have no guiding principles. Our personal values and virtues are that inner compass. They keep us oriented toward what truly matters, no matter which way the storm blows. As the speaker Jim Rohn wisely put it, *"It is our philosophical set of the sail that determines the course of our lives. To change our current direction, we have to change our philosophy, not our circumstances."* In other words, if **you** don't decide what you stand for, the world will decide for you — and that's a risky way to live.

When I was younger, I learned this the hard way. I had no clear values of my own; I simply went whichever way the breeze of circumstance blew me. One day I chased success, the next day I chased approval — and I never felt truly satisfied. I was like that ship with no compass, carried by currents I didn't choose. It wasn't until life's waves nearly wrecked me that I realized I needed an **anchor**. I needed to deliberately choose the principles that would ground me. Here's a simple truth I discovered: when you stand for nothing, you'll fall for anything. By contrast, living by your own principles gives you stability. It builds self-respect, because each day you *know* why you do what you do. It's incredibly empowering to say, "I choose this path because it aligns with my values," rather than, "I do this because everyone else does."

TOOLKIT REFERENCE *To begin exploring your own guiding principles, see "Values Exploration Exercise" and "Life Moments Analysis" in Section 2 of the Practical Toolkit.*

Different thinkers throughout history have offered their own lists of ideal virtues to live by. There's no one-size-fits-all set, and I'm not here to hand you a strict rulebook.

Instead, consider this chapter an exploration of wisdom — a kind of philosophical buffet. We'll sample ideas from ancient philosophy and modern thought, and you can take what resonates. Remember the advice often attributed to Bruce Lee: *"Absorb what is useful, discard what is not, add what is uniquely your own."* In the end, the compass you craft will be uniquely yours, a blend of timeless insight and personal truth.

Ancient Guides: The Stoic Virtues

My journey in defining my principles began with an old book of **Stoic philosophy** I picked up in a second-hand shop. The Stoics — sages from ancient Greece and Rome — taught that a well-lived life rests on four cardinal virtues. These are timeless principles, as steady in the 21st century as they were two thousand years ago. I remember sitting in a quiet corner of a café, turning the pages and discovering these four pillars of character. They immediately struck a chord. I imagined what each virtue might look like if I applied it to my modern life.

Wisdom (Prudence): The Stoics saw wisdom not as IQ or trivia knowledge, but as practical good sense — the ability to discern the important from the trivial, to see the big picture, and to make sound decisions. I realized wisdom could be as simple as the moment I *pause* before reacting in anger, or the humility to learn from a mistake. It's that inner voice of reason that says, "Is this action aligned with my goals and values?" before I act. Wisdom became, for me, taking a breath and choosing response over reflex. The philosopher Epictetus taught that we must discern what is within our control and what is not — focusing only on what we *can* change. I found a profound peace in this. I couldn't control the past, or other people's choices, or sudden storms in life, but I could control *my* actions and attitudes. That realization was like seeing a lighthouse through the fog.

TOOLKIT REFERENCE*To develop practical wisdom in everyday decisions, explore the "Controllable vs. Uncontrollable Sorting" and "Pause Practice" exercises in Section 2 of the Practical Toolkit.*

Courage (Fortitude): Not just physical bravery, but moral courage — doing the right thing even when it's hard or when fear is telling you to back down. Life will test us, the Stoics knew, whether it's speaking up against wrongdoing or persevering through tough times. Reading about courage, I recalled moments in my own life where I *did* the easier thing instead of the right thing, out of fear. I decided I didn't want to live that way anymore. *"Sometimes even to live is an act of courage,"* wrote Seneca, the Roman Stoic. That line hit me deep. It reminded me that simply facing each day — getting out of bed when despair weighs you down, or stepping outside your comfort zone — can be a brave act. Courage, I learned, is built through **daily** acts of bravery: having that difficult conversation I've been avoiding, resisting negative peer pressure, or pursuing a dream that scares me. Every time we act in spite of fear, we grow in strength. I started striving to live with that kind of everyday courage.

Justice (Fairness): To the Stoics, justice meant integrity, fairness, and kindness in our interactions. It's treating others honorably and giving each person their due. I thought about what justice meant in my life — it could be as simple as keeping my promises, or as challenging as standing up for someone being treated unfairly. Marcus Aurelius, the philosopher-emperor, put it beautifully: *"What's bad for the hive is bad for the bee."* In other words, we're all part of a community; if I hurt others, I ultimately hurt myself, too. True justice considers the greater good. I began to see that living with justice isn't only about big social causes; it's also in the small, everyday choices of honesty and respect. For instance, if I expect honesty or loyalty from a friend, I must practice those virtues myself. Justice in my compass became a reminder that my actions affect not just me but those around me — and that I want those effects to be positive and fair.

Temperance (Self-Control): The art of balance, moderation, and self-control. In an age of instant gratification, this virtue felt especially relevant — and challenging. Temperance is about managing our desires and impulses so they don't control us. I smiled reading the Stoics' take on it, because it felt like they were speaking directly to our modern temptations. One commentator described temperance as protection from extremes: not too much, not too little. I recalled many nights binging far too many episodes of a show or indulging in junk food until I felt sick. To practice temperance is not to reject enjoyment, but to **savor** it in the right amount. It might mean having one slice of cake and truly enjoying it, instead of devouring the whole thing and regretting it. Or it could mean exercising restraint when angry, rather than lashing out. I started to see temperance as a form of self-respect: by exercising control, I was caring for my long-term well-being instead of surrendering to momentary whims. Anything worthwhile — health, relationships, even knowledge — thrives in balance.

TOOLKIT REFERENCE *To strengthen your ability to show temperance in daily life, practice the "Delayed Gratification Exercise" and "Mindful Consumption Tracking" in Section 2 of the Practical Toolkit.*

Figure 1: The Four Stoic Virtues and how they complement each other to create a balanced character.

Taken together, these four virtues of Stoicism — wisdom, courage, justice, temperance — gave me a sturdy framework, like the four points of a compass. A person who cultivates these virtues, I realized, will likely find an inner strength and steadiness no matter what life throws at them. Because if your guiding principle in any situation is to respond with wisdom, with courage, with fairness, with self-control — then you have something solid to rely on: your **character**. Even if the outcome is uncertain, you can trust yourself to navigate it honorably.

It was also comforting to know I didn't have to be perfect. Nobody is. Even the Stoics admitted that the perfectly virtuous person is an unattainable ideal. I certainly wasn't going to transform overnight into some kind of sage who never slips up. But that's not the point. The point is to have something to aspire to — a North Star to guide you when you're unsure. The purpose of a compass isn't to make you perfect; it's to keep you moving toward *true north*. If I strayed off course, I could correct it. If I failed to live up to my values one day, I could try again the next. Knowing my principles gave me a way to course-correct rather than just feel lost in guilt or confusion.

"Your values are like a personal GPS system — they won't prevent you from taking wrong turns, but they'll always help you find your way back." — Original

Honesty: True North of the Soul

As I reflected on the Stoic four virtues, I realized something was still missing *for me*. There was another value, not explicitly on the ancient list, that had to be the **bedrock** of my compass: **Honesty**. In truth, honesty is woven through the other virtues (you can't have justice without honesty, or even real courage), but I felt it deserved its own spotlight. Honesty means living in truth — with others *and* with yourself. It's the opposite of living in illusion or half-truths. And in my experience, honesty is the foundation upon which all the other virtues stand. You cannot be wise if you refuse to see the facts. You cannot be just if you deceive others. You cannot be courageous if you're hiding from the truth.

I learned the importance of honesty through one of the most painful and liberating chapters of my life. There was a time when I lived a kind of double life — presenting one face to the world while knowing that reality was very different. I told lies to people I cared about. Worst of all, I lied to myself about who I was and what I was doing. I chased quick rewards and ignored my conscience. Each lie I told dug me deeper into a hole of anxiety and guilt. I was always looking over my shoulder, waiting for my facades to crumble. And they did. Eventually the weight of my own dishonesty became unbearable. I felt divided against myself — as if there were two me's: the false image I projected, and the real me, suffocating underneath. Every day lived in dishonesty made me feel more fragile, fearful, **weak**.

Why weak? Because dishonesty is born of fear — fear of the truth. It's been said that *"honesty is an act of courage,"* and I believe that wholeheartedly. Telling the truth, especially when the truth is unwelcome or hard, requires bravery. I remember the night I hit rock bottom. I was alone, staring at the mirror, hardly recognizing myself. I realized I couldn't stand what I saw: a coward hiding behind lies. In that moment, something shifted. I decided that no matter the consequences, I had to start living truthfully. I began confessing the secrets I'd been keeping. I owned up to my mistakes. I faced the hurt I had caused. It was one of the hardest things I've ever done — my heart pounded, my hands literally trembled as I made phone calls and had face-to-face conversations that scared me to death. But with each admission, I felt a small piece of my self-respect return.

TOOLKIT REFERENCE *For a guided process to strengthen your honesty with yourself and others, see "Truth-Telling Inventory" and "Confession Practice" in Section 2 of the Practical Toolkit.*

Choosing honesty was like realigning my compass to true north after it had been demagnetized by lies. The change in my life was immediate and profound. Suddenly, the other virtues became attainable again: I could exercise wisdom because I wasn't distorting reality to suit a lie; I found courage because I was no longer hiding from my fears; I pursued justice because I cared about doing right by people rather than covering my tracks. And perhaps most importantly, I could look at myself in the mirror again and *not flinch*. There's a saying I came across around that time: "A clear conscience is the softest pillow." I discovered how true that is. When my head hit the pillow at night, I could finally relax, knowing I wasn't running from anything anymore.

Since that turning point, I've made honesty a non-negotiable core of my compass. It doesn't mean I never slip or avoid truth — I'm human — but it means I strive, always, to return to honesty as my baseline. Being truthful in words and actions, and also being brutally honest with myself in self-reflection. No more fooling myself with convenient excuses or rationalizations. If something in my life isn't working, I acknowledge it. If I have a dream or desire I've been afraid to admit, I confront it. Honesty clarifies; it's like cleaning a smudged window so that you can see the world outside clearly. When you live truthfully, you gain clarity about who you are, and a peace in knowing that who you *appear* to be is who you truly **are**. By anchoring myself in honesty, I ensure that my entire moral compass isn't built on sand. All the other principles hold strong only if they're rooted in truth.

"The hardest truth spoken aloud will free you more than the prettiest lie kept silent." — Original

In sharing this, I encourage you to consider making honesty a foundational virtue in *your* compass as well. It's not easy — being honest with oneself can be as challenging as being honest with others — but it is deeply rewarding. With honesty guiding you, you can trust yourself. Your inner voice gets louder and clearer. You gain a quiet confidence, because you know that no matter what mistakes you might make, you won't lie to escape them. You will face life head-on. That resolve is a source of real strength.

Honesty in Practice: Questions for Self-Examination

Before moving forward, consider these questions to gauge your relationship with honesty:

1. What truths am I currently avoiding in my life?

2. Where do I present a version of myself that doesn't align with who I really am?

3. What would change if I were completely honest with myself about my strengths and weaknesses?

4. What one step toward greater honesty could I take this week?

5. Who in my life embodies authentic honesty, and what can I learn from them?

Freedom and Responsibility: An Existential Perspective

Defining my values through wisdom, courage, justice, temperance, and honesty gave me an anchor of ancient wisdom. But I also came to realize I needed **direction** — a sense of meaning and purpose that *I* chose for myself. Here, a very different school of thought illuminated my path: **Existentialism**. If Stoicism provided the stars by which to navigate, existentialism taught me that *I* am the navigator. It reminded me that no one else can define my life for me — I have to define it myself.

In my search for guidance, I picked up Viktor Frankl's memoir *Man's Search for Meaning*. Frankl was a psychiatrist who survived the horrors of Auschwitz in World War II. What I read in that book moved me to my core. Frankl observed that even in the most painful, uncontrollable circumstances, people could endure almost anything **if they held onto a purpose**. Amid unimaginable suffering, those who had a reason — whether it was love for someone, faith in something, or a goal waiting beyond the barbed wire — were more likely to survive each day. That insight forever changed how I view life's hardships.

It taught me that meaning is not a luxury; it's a lifeline. We can face the worst if we know *why*.

TOOLKIT REFERENCE *To discover your own sense of meaning and purpose, explore the "Personal Meaning Map" and "Three Whys Deep" exercises in Section 2 of the Practical Toolkit.*

Frankl's words echo a famous line by Nietzsche: "He who has a *why* to live can bear almost any *how*." Frankl embodied this. He wrote that *"Ultimately, man should not ask what the meaning of his life is, but rather must recognize that it is he who is asked... he can only answer to life by answering for his own life."* In the wreckage of a world that had taken everything from him, Frankl realized that life was still asking *him* for meaning, and that no one else could answer that question for him. This was an astonishing perspective: to turn the question around and see ourselves as responsible for giving life meaning, rather than passively seeking meaning out there. It means that **your life is a question, and *you* are the answer**.

Around the same time, I delved into the essays of Jean-Paul Sartre, one of the key existentialist philosophers. Sartre's ideas were challenging but exhilarating. He famously declared, *"Life has no meaning a priori... It is up to you to give it a meaning, and value is nothing but the meaning that you choose."* When I first read that, it felt a bit like being doused in cold water — shocking and bracing. Sartre wasn't saying life is meaningless in a nihilistic way; he was saying meaning isn't handed to us at birth. There is no pre-written script, no default purpose waiting. We are free to choose—and with that freedom comes the weighty responsibility to choose well. Sartre even said that humans are *"condemned to be free"* — condemned because we *must* make choices in life, there's no escape from this freedom. Not choosing is itself a choice, one that leads to drifting and letting circumstances write your story. I found this idea daunting and liberating at once. If I had absolute freedom to define my values and purpose, then I could no longer blame society or my parents or chance for who I became. **I was the author of my own life.**

Taken together, Frankl and Sartre gave me a powerful message: No one *else* can tell you what your life means, or what principles should guide you. **You** have to decide. You have to *choose* your North Stars and then follow them. This is self-authorship — recognizing that if life were a book, you are the one holding the pen. The world will throw plot twists at you outside your control, yes. But within whatever context you find yourself, you get to decide the character you'll be and what that character stands for. This realization was intimidating (because I couldn't fall back on "fate" or others to shape my destiny) but it was also exhilarating and empowering. It meant that no matter what had happened before, I could pick up the pen *today* and write a new chapter, redefine my values, change my direction.

"**In the space between what happens to you and how you respond lies your greatest power: the freedom to choose who you become.**" — Original

Choosing Your North Star Principles

With the wisdom of the Stoics giving me a **moral foundation** and the existentialists reminding me of my **freedom to choose**, I set out to consciously build my own compass. I asked myself: *What do I want my guiding principles to be?* What virtues or values feel so essential to me that I want to live by them every day?

This turned out to be a deeply personal and illuminating exercise. I remember one quiet evening, I sat at my kitchen table with a notebook, determined to jot down the values that resonated with me. At first, I wrote a long, rambling list of every good quality I could think of: **kindness, creativity, humility, discipline, faith, generosity, curiosity**, and so on. The list spilled over the page, a reflection of all the virtues various teachers and traditions had extolled. But I knew I couldn't possibly focus on twenty different values all at once in life. I needed to hone in on the core ones — the ones that felt like *me*, that inspired me, that I aspired to even if I often fell short.

To narrow it down, I began reflecting on a few key questions, almost like a conversation with myself. I considered **the people I admired most** in the world and in my life. What qualities did they embody? Immediately I thought of my grandfather — a man of unwavering integrity and warmth — and realized how much I prize **kindness** and **honesty** because of him. I thought of a close friend who is fearlessly **authentic** and always speaks her mind, and I knew I valued that kind of authenticity and courage. I even thought of famous figures — like I've always admired how Viktor Frankl held onto **hope** and meaning, or how Marcus Aurelius exemplified **self-discipline** and wisdom. These reflections started highlighting values that rang true to me.

TOOLKIT REFERENCE *To identify your unique core values, use the "Values from Admiration" and "Decision History Analysis" exercises in Section 2 of the Practical Toolkit.*

Next, I asked: **When have I felt most proud of myself?** I sifted through memories and found a few shining moments that stood out. In each of them, I realized, I had been living a value that mattered. I felt proud the day I stood up for a colleague who was being treated unfairly — that was me honoring **justice**. I felt at peace the time I forgave someone who hurt me, rather than holding a grudge — that was me practicing **compassion** and understanding. I felt a quiet pride when I finished a difficult project by sticking with it despite wanting to quit — that was **perseverance**. These moments of pride were like a compass needle quivering toward my true values.

I also thought about **what values I expect from others** in my relationships, because that can be a mirror of what I hold important. I knew I cannot tolerate dishonesty in a friend — which underscored how crucial **honesty** is to me. I deeply value friends who are **loyal** and **empathetic**, which told me loyalty and empathy are part of my own creed. And I considered, if I were to have children or mentor someone young, **what guiding principles would I want to instill in them?** The answer to that question came from a very pure place in my heart — I would want them to be kind, to be curious, to have integrity, to work hard and treat people fairly. In advising an imaginary child, I inadvertently revealed to myself what I believe is *truly* important in life.

Slowly, through this introspection, my long list of virtues narrowed to a handful of core values that felt authentic to me. I circled five of them. There was a bit of overlap with the Stoic big four, but my list also reflected my unique journey. I had **Honesty**, of course, at the top — my hard-won north star. I included **Courage**, because I knew fear had too often held me back. **Kindness** made the list; I realized that showing warmth and compassion gave my life meaning and joy. **Growth** (or learning) was there, as I've always felt life is an adventure of learning and I never want to stagnate. And **Responsibility** found its way in — the sense that I must take responsibility for my choices, echoing that existential lesson of self-authorship. These five would be my guiding stars, my personal constellation to navigate by.

I want to emphasize something: there is no *right* number of core values to have, and they can evolve as you do. I started with around five because it was a manageable number that I could remember and actually try to live by each day. More than that, and I knew I'd be overwhelmed or forget to honor some. Fewer, and I might be oversimplifying myself. Five felt right. Your number might be three or seven or any number that suits you — what matters is that they truly **mean** something to you. Also, choosing these values isn't like etching words into stone for all eternity. Life changes us. Ten years ago, I might not have put "honesty" on my list — shamefully, it took my personal crash to see its importance. And perhaps in the future, another value will emerge as key for me. That's okay. Your compass can be refined over time. The goal is to be *conscious* and *deliberate* about what guides you, rather than drifting on autopilot.

TOOLKIT REFERENCE *To help articulate and refine your final list of core values, complete the "Personal Values Statement" and "Values Prioritization Matrix" in Section 2 of the Practical Toolkit.*

Once I had my compass points defined, something interesting happened. I began to feel a new sense of agency and clarity in day-to-day life. When faced with decisions, big or small, I had a reference point: *Does this choice align with my values?* Decisions that used to torment me with doubt suddenly became clearer. If an option would require me to compromise my honesty or responsibility, I knew it wasn't the right path. If a course of action allowed me to express kindness or required courage, I felt drawn to it even if it was hard, because I knew it fit the kind of person I wanted to be. It's as if I had given myself a filter for life, and through it I could see which endeavors were *greenlights* (go for it) and which were *red flags*.

I also noticed an inner harmony growing. Living in alignment with your values does something powerful: it reduces the internal conflict and stress that come from acting against your own conscience. Modern psychology backs this up—studies have shown that people who pursue goals aligned with their personal values experience greater life satisfaction and less stress, whereas chasing goals that conflict with one's core values can lead to emptiness or burnout. I certainly found this to be true. When my actions reflected my beliefs, I felt a sense of integrity and peace that I'd never felt during my rudderless years. I started respecting myself more, and interestingly, I think others sensed this change in me as well. Friends and colleagues saw that I was more consistent and principled, and as a result I earned their trust in a deeper way. After all, when someone clearly stands for something, you know where they stand, and that builds respect.

"When your actions align with your values, you walk with the quiet confidence of someone who knows exactly who they are." — Original

Of course, none of this means I became a saint overnight. Far from it! I continued to encounter moments of temptation, laziness, or fear where I'd slip up and act contrary to my values. I'm as fallibly human as anyone. But now, I had a way to right the ship when it listed off course. I'd reflect on what went wrong, remind myself of why that value matters, and correct my behavior. I came to think of my principles as a **lighthouse on a foggy shore** — I might drift from the path, but I could always reorient myself when I saw the light. In practical terms, I used tools like journaling to stay aligned. If I lost my temper (betraying my value of kindness or self-control), I'd write about it at night and unpack what triggered me, then visualize how I'd handle it better next time. If I caught myself rationalizing something shady at work (nudging against honesty), I'd recognize that discomfort as the alarm bell it was, and promptly change course. In this way, my compass kept me honest (literally!) and accountable. It wasn't about never failing; it was about having a guide to *return to* when I did fail.

Living Your Values, Day by Day

Defining values is one thing, but living by them is another. I knew that if I wanted these beautiful principles to truly shape my life, I needed to practice them consistently. So, I made a personal challenge. I decided that for one week, I would consciously **live one core value each day** and observe what happened. It was a kind of experiment in character-building — a way to turn theory into practice.

On Monday, I focused on **Honesty**. That day, I vowed to be completely truthful and open in all my interactions — and importantly, to be honest with myself about my feelings and motivations. I remember I finally had a frank, heartfelt conversation with a friend that I'd been putting off for months. I admitted to a mistake at work instead of quietly sweeping it under the rug. It wasn't easy, but that night I felt an unexpected relief and pride.

Tuesday was dedicated to **Courage**. I'm naturally someone who has had a lot of fears — some big, some small. I decided that day I would do at least one thing that scared me. I ended up volunteering to lead a team meeting that I usually would shy away from. My voice shook a little, but I did it. I also spoke up in a situation where I felt someone was being treated unfairly, whereas the old me might have stayed silent. By the end of the day, I had a little spark inside, a realization: *I can do this*. Courage is like a muscle — it grows when you use it.

TOOLKIT REFERENCE *To turn your abstract values into daily practices, use the "Value-to-Action Bridge" and "Weekly Value Focus Plan" in Section 2 of the Practical Toolkit.*

Wednesday, I chose **Kindness** as my focus. I tried to go through the day looking for opportunities to be kind, even in small ways. I struck up a friendly conversation with the lonely-looking security guard in our building, bought coffee for a coworker who was having a rough morning, and in the evening, I called my mother just to tell her I appreciated her. These weren't grand gestures, but I found they lifted *my* spirits as much as anyone else's. I went to bed feeling oddly content, like I had been the person I truly want to be.

Later in the week, I practiced **Discipline** (tackling my exercise routine and paperwork with diligence instead of procrastination) and **Gratitude** (taking note of all the things I was thankful for throughout the day). Each day had its challenges; some values came more naturally, others required real effort. But every day taught me something new about myself. By Sunday, when I reflected on the week, I noticed a few changes. I felt more **centered** and confident. There was a quiet happiness in knowing I had spent my week in line with what I professed to care about. It was as if I had been "walking my talk," and that congruence between my insides and outsides gave me strength. I realized that all the little choices we make—choosing honesty in a single conversation, choosing patience in a single moment of irritation—add up to our character over time. Character isn't built in a day; it's built by small choices made daily. And each day that you live by your compass, you reinforce those guiding principles within you, until they become second nature.

I've continued this practice beyond that week, making it a lifelong habit. I often start my morning by thinking of my core values and setting a simple intention: *How can I express one of these values today?* It might be a tiny action, but it keeps the compass aligned. And at night, I often do a quick mental scan of my day: *Did I live my values? Where did I fall short? What can I try differently tomorrow?* This isn't about beating myself up; it's about continuous growth. Some days I give myself a mental high-five because I *did* act with integrity or courage when it was tough. Other days, I sigh because I gave in to an old habit or fear, but then I remind myself tomorrow is a new chance to do better.

"Values aren't meant to be framed on a wall; they're meant to be lived in the trenches of ordinary days." — Original

Over time, living by my compass has transformed my life in subtle but profound ways. Decisions are easier, because now I have an internal *yes/no* filter: if a choice doesn't fit my values, I know it's not right for me. I've also noticed that I worry less about what others think or what the "trends" say I should do. I have my own measuring stick. Paradoxically, by focusing on *being* a better person rather than on what I have or achieve, I've achieved more of the things I actually care about. And I experience a sense of peace, a feeling of being at home with myself, that I never had when I was trying to live by others' standards.

Values-Based Decision Making Checklist

When facing a significant choice, ask yourself:

- Does this option align with my core values? Which ones specifically?

- Will this decision require me to compromise any of my values?

- How will I feel about this choice a year from now?

- Would I be comfortable if others knew I made this choice?

- Does this decision move me toward becoming the person I want to be?

- If I were advising someone I love, what would I tell them to do?

In closing, I want to share one more image that stays with me: **your values are like the roots of a great tree**. They might be mostly invisible to the world, underground, but they are what give you strength and nourishment. Storms will inevitably come in life — fierce winds of change, torrents of adversity — but if your roots go deep, you will stand tall through it all. In fact, you won't just withstand the storms; you'll grow because of them, reaching higher in the sunshine and rain alike. By choosing your guiding principles and tending to them, you take charge of your life's direction. You become the captain of your ship, steering confidently by the stars *you* chose, rather than a passenger swept this way and that by the tides. On rough days, your compass will help you navigate, keeping you from despair or from betraying yourself. On good days, it will remind you to be grateful and humble, because those too are part of your values.

TOOLKIT REFERENCE *To sustain your values over time, practice the "Values Review Ritual" and "Course Correction Questions" in Section 2 of the Practical Toolkit.*

So build your compass, and carry it with you. Let it guide your decisions and actions. When you do, watch how life changes. Instead of living by default, you start living by design — a design you crafted, guided by timeless wisdom and your own honest reflection. One day, you'll look back on this journey of self-discovery and perhaps realize that your future self is quietly smiling, grateful that you chose to live **authentically**. Every step you take on this path is an act of self-authorship, an answer to the question of life's meaning that only you can give. And that, I believe, is a truly heroic journey to undertake. Your future self will thank you for it.

Bridge to Chapter 3: From Values to Discipline

Having established your internal compass—the core values and principles that will guide your life—we now face a crucial question: How do we translate these noble intentions into consistent action? After all, knowing your values is one thing; living by them day after day is quite another.

This brings us to our next essential step in the journey of self-development: the power of **daily discipline**. In Chapter 3, we'll explore how to build habits and routines that align with your values, turning your compass into a roadmap of consistent action. We'll discover why discipline isn't about rigid control but about freedom—the freedom to become who you truly want to be.

Just as a ship with a compass still needs sails and a steady hand on the rudder to reach its destination, your values need the supporting force of discipline to manifest in your life. Together, these elements—knowing your direction and having the discipline to move steadily toward it—create an unstoppable momentum of personal growth.

As we turn the page to "Brick by Brick: The Power of Daily Discipline," prepare to discover how small, consistent actions build the bridge between who you are and who you aspire to become. Your compass is set; now let's learn to follow it faithfully, one disciplined step at a time.

3

BRICK BY BRICK — THE POWER OF DAILY DISCIPLINE

"You are not what you say you are — you are what you do every single day."

It was past midnight and Alex sat alone in the glow of his desk lamp, staring at an almost empty journal. Another day had slipped by, and once again he had broken the little promises he made to himself. That morning he *swore* he would get up at 6:00 AM to exercise, but he hit the snooze button three times. He *intended* to write in his journal before bed, but here he was, exhausted and disappointed, with nothing written. The pattern wasn't new. Alex often told friends (and himself) how motivated he was to improve — yet his daily actions painted a different story. As he flipped through the journal's sparse pages, a quote he'd jotted down months ago caught his eye, etched in blue ink and determination:

"You are not what you say you are — you are what you do every single day."

The words hit him like a jolt. In that quiet moment, Alex felt the sting of truth. He realized he'd been **all talk and no action**, making grand plans but not following through. It dawned on him that every time he broke a promise to himself — no matter how small — he was telling his subconscious *"I don't really mean what I say."* His confidence was eroding one snooze, one skipped workout, one empty journal page at a time. A lump caught in his throat as he asked himself: *If I'm not even honest with myself, how can I have any self-respect?*

But there was another feeling in that moment too — a flicker of hope. Alex understood that if breaking promises chipped away at self-trust, then **keeping** promises, even tiny ones, could start to rebuild it. He closed his eyes and made a simple, powerful vow: starting tomorrow, he would **keep his promises to himself**, one by one, brick by brick. It wouldn't matter if they were small — waking up when the alarm rang, writing *one* *paragraph* in his journal, drinking water instead of soda — he would do what he said he would do. That night Alex turned a page in his life story. Instead of *saying* who he wanted to be, he would *prove* it through daily action. In the silence, he felt something new: a sense that he could trust himself again.

TOOLKIT REFERENCE *To begin establishing self-trust through kept promises, see the "Daily Integrity Tracker" and "Promise-Keeping Practice" in Section 3 of the Practical Toolkit.*

The Promise to Yourself — Foundation of Self-Discipline

Alex's late-night epiphany highlights a fundamental truth: **the promises you keep to yourself are the foundation of a disciplined life.** Each small commitment kept is like a brick in the building of your character, a deposit into your self-esteem. Over time, those bricks form an unshakable foundation. *Each time you honor your word to yourself — getting up with the alarm, finishing that workout, making that difficult phone call — you reinforce the belief that you are reliable.* You send yourself the message, "I can trust me." And that is a powerful message.

Conversely, every time you break a self-promise, it chips away at that foundation. Hitting snooze when you vowed to rise early may seem trivial, but in that moment you're telling yourself that your own plans don't matter. Do it often, and an erosion of self-trust begins. You start doubting your willpower and even your worth. Think about it: *Have you ever repeatedly told yourself you'd do something and then didn't?* Most of us have, and it never feels good. There's a gnawing disappointment that lingers — not because skipping one workout or one study session is catastrophic in itself, but because it's a **betrayal of the self**.

"Every time you honor a commitment to yourself, you build a relationship of trust with the most important person in your life—you." — Original

Famed Stoic philosopher Marcus Aurelius warned, *"Waste no more time arguing about what a good man should be. **Be one**."* In other words, stop telling yourself (and others) what you *will* do and just **do it**. Actions, not words, reveal who you truly are. Alex recognized this. He saw that to respect himself, he had to **live** his values and goals, not just talk about them. The next morning, when the alarm rang, he remembered his promise. He groaned, felt the familiar temptation to stay in bed... but then he swung his legs out and *stood up*. That single act — getting up when he said he would — was his first **victory** of the day. It was tiny, but it mattered.

Keeping that one promise gave Alex a spark of pride. As the days went on, he kept stringing together these small wins. He'd tell himself to write for five minutes, and he did. He'd promise to drink water each morning, and he did. Each success was a **vote of confidence** for his new self. Instead of quietly quitting on himself, he started quietly **believing** in himself. It showed him first-hand what one mentor had told him: *Success is nothing more than a few simple disciplines, practiced every day.*

"Discipline is the bridge between goals and accomplishment." — **Jim Rohn**

The bridge Jim Rohn speaks of is built on those daily kept promises. Every promise kept is a plank laid on that bridge, carrying you from where you are to where you want to be. So ask yourself right now: **What is one promise you've made to yourself recently that you haven't kept?** It could be as small as going to bed earlier, or calling a friend you've been meaning to, or staying consistent with a class or hobby. How did you feel when you didn't follow through? Now imagine the pride you'd feel if you *had* kept that promise — not just once, but every day for a week, a month. *Pause and picture it.* That feeling of pride and self-respect is within reach, and it starts with keeping **one small promise** today.

TOOLKIT REFERENCE *To strengthen your ability to keep self-promises, practice the "Promise Hierarchy Method" and "Minimum Viable Commitment" exercises in Section 3 of the Practical Toolkit.*

Discipline Over Motivation — Lighting the Steady Fire

Motivation is a wonderful feeling — that surge of inspiration when you watch an uplifting video or hear an energizing speech. It's the spark that can get you excited about making a change. The trouble is, motivation is like the wind: it comes and goes on its own schedule. You might wake up on Monday full of motivation, ready to conquer the world, and by Wednesday that excitement has fizzled out. We can't *control* when we feel motivated; it's a fickle friend. If you rely solely on motivation to take action, you'll only do what you need to do when you "feel like it." And as anyone who has tried to achieve a big goal knows, waiting until you **feel** like it is a recipe for inconsistency.

Discipline, on the other hand, is like a steady flame — *less flashy than a spark, but far more reliable.* **Discipline doesn't depend on your mood or energy level; it's a choice to stick to your plan even on the days you *don't* feel inspired.** Think about a skilled sailor: they can't control the wind, but they have mastered the art of adjusting their sails. You too have learned to adjust your sails.

"Discipline is the decision to choose what you want most over what you want now." — Original

One of Alex's biggest realizations was that he could perform his morning run or his journaling ritual *even if* he wasn't brimming with enthusiasm at that moment. He learned that some days you simply start with a sense of duty, and that's okay. Paradoxically, once you get going, the **action** itself often generates a bit of motivation to help you continue. As the saying goes, "Mood follows action." That is, don't wait for the mood to strike — start doing something and your mindset will catch up.

Remember: *"Motivation is what gets you started. **Habit** is what keeps you going."* This popular quote (often attributed to Jim Rohn) rings true — an initial burst of inspiration can kickstart a journey, but it's the disciplined habits that carry you to the finish line. Think of an elite athlete, a successful entrepreneur, or even a consistently healthy person you admire. Are they fired up with motivation every single day? Probably not. What they have cultivated is discipline — the ability to do what must be done *even when* they don't want to. They've trained that discipline like a muscle, and it kicks in automatically.

Jim Rohn also summed up the stake of this choice in a powerful way:

"We must all suffer one of two pains: the pain of discipline or the pain of regret. The difference is that discipline weighs ounces while regret weighs tons." — **Jim Rohn**

Take a moment to let that sink in. The *pain of discipline* is the discomfort of doing the hard thing now — waking up early on a cold morning to go jogging, saying no to a second slice of cake, sitting down to study when you'd rather watch TV. That pain is real, but it's mild and it passes quickly. In contrast, the *pain of regret* is what you feel later, when weeks or months have passed and you're no closer to your goals because you continually gave in to ease. Regret is the heavy burden of knowing you **could have** been better, if only you had been more disciplined.

TOOLKIT REFERENCE *To build your discipline muscles, practice the "Discomfort Training" and "Action-First Protocol" in Section 3 of the Practical Toolkit.*

When Alex started choosing discipline over motivation, he experienced that first type of pain — the sting of cold morning air on his jog, the soreness of muscles getting used to exercise, the mental effort of focusing on writing for 10 minutes instead of scrolling on his phone. But with each challenge he pushed through, it was like a small sacrifice in exchange for a *big reward*: he ended his days with pride instead of guilt. He began to say, *"I choose the pain of discipline now, so I never have to feel the pain of regret later."* In doing so, he discovered a liberating truth: **discipline is actually a form of freedom**. It frees you from being a slave to fluctuating feelings. It frees you from later remorse. It puts you in control of your path.

By cultivating discipline, you become the master of your commitments. You act based on your values and decisions, not based on which way the wind of motivation is blowing today. This doesn't mean you become a robot — it means you carry on with your plan kindly, *whether or not* you woke up in a good mood. And an interesting thing happens when you do this consistently: you start to take pride in your ability to show up, and your self-confidence grows. Others may even start asking, *"How do you stay so motivated?"* And you might smile, because you know the secret is not motivation at all — **it's habit and discipline**.

Discipline is the steady fire that burns long after motivation's spark has faded. Feed that fire, and it will warm you with results and self-respect. The next time you catch yourself thinking, *"I just don't feel motivated,"* treat it as a gentle alarm bell. That's your cue to lean on discipline. Do it *anyway*. You can feel completely unmotivated and still take one small step forward — whether it's one set of exercise, one page of reading, or one difficult conversation. Ironically, once you start, you'll often find motivation swooping back in to join you. And if not, no matter — you're still getting it done.

Overcoming Initial Resistance to Action

For many of us, the hardest part of discipline is overcoming that initial wall of resistance that appears just before we begin. Here are strategies that work for different personality types:

For Analytical Types:

- Set a timer for just 5 minutes and commit to starting. This makes the task feel finite and manageable.

- Break the task into extremely small components and check them off one by one.

- Track your discipline metrics (like days in a row) to satisfy your need for data and progress.

For Creative Types:

- Create a ritual that makes starting feel special (special music, a particular candle, a specific location).

- Connect the disciplined action to a larger purpose or meaning that excites you.

- Allow yourself to approach the task in a non-linear way that feels more natural to your thinking style.

For Socially-Motivated Types:

- Find an accountability partner or group where you check in regularly.

- Make public commitments about your intentions.

- Share your progress with others who will celebrate your consistency.

For Comfort-Seekers:

- Create an environment that minimizes discomfort around the task (comfortable clothes, pleasant temperature, etc.).

- Pair the disciplined action with something enjoyable (like listening to a favorite podcast while exercising).

- Focus on how much better you'll feel after completing the task, rather than how uncomfortable starting might be.

Whatever your personality type, remember that resistance is normal, not a sign that you lack willpower. Expect it, plan for it, and develop your personal strategy for moving through it.

Consistency Over Intensity — The Slow, Steady Path to Greatness

In our fast-paced world, it's easy to get caught up in the excitement of dramatic gestures. We dream of overnight transformations: going from couch potato to marathon runner in a week, or binge-studying for an exam in one all-nighter to make up for weeks of procrastination. However, when it comes to real, lasting change, **consistency beats intensity** every time. It's the classic tortoise and hare story: slow and steady truly wins the race.

Imagine two friends, Alice and Bob, who both decide to expand their knowledge by reading. Alice sets a humble goal to read *one chapter* (about 10 pages) of a book every single day. Bob, bursting with enthusiasm, picks up a 300-page book and plows through 70 pages in one sitting on a Sunday afternoon. Who's doing more? On that day, Bob certainly *appears* more impressive — 70 pages is a lot. But what happens next? Bob finds it hard to fit reading into his busy weekdays, so he doesn't read again for another week or two, maybe when another surge of motivation strikes. Alice, on the other hand, makes reading a daily ritual — 10 pages each evening without fail, perhaps as part of her bedtime wind-down. After one month, Alice has read roughly 300 pages (10 pages × 30 days), likely completing one or two books. Bob managed 70 pages twice, totaling 140 pages, and then lost momentum. After six months, Alice has hundreds of pages — a dozen books — under her belt, while Bob, despite his sporadic bursts, has finished maybe a book or two at most. Alice's gentle daily habit vastly outpaces Bob's intense-but-infrequent approach.

"Greatness isn't built in a day of heroic effort, but in a thousand days of showing up when nobody's watching." — Original

This scenario plays out in all areas of life. Whether it's exercise, studying, saving money, or practicing a skill, **small daily improvements add up to stunning results over time**. As leadership expert Robin Sharma reminds us:

"Small daily improvements over time lead to stunning results." — **Robin Sharma**

TOOLKIT REFERENCE *To embed consistency into your routine, try the "Minimum Daily Practice" and "Habit Streaking" techniques in Section 3 of the Practical Toolkit.*

The power of consistency comes from the magic of compounding. Just as money in a bank can earn interest and grow exponentially, your habits compound. Doing 10 push-ups a day might not make you feel like a bodybuilder in the moment, but 10 push-ups daily for a year is 3,650 push-ups — that *will* change your strength and body. Writing 200 words a day seems minor, but in a year that's 73,000 words — nearly a novel. Tiny actions, repeated, have tremendous force. Intensity, on the other hand, is like a fireworks show — dazzling one moment and gone the next. Consistency is the sunrise every single morning — reliable and life-giving.

Consistency also creates **momentum**. When you do something every day, it starts to feel like a natural part of your routine — almost automatic. You spend less energy debating whether to do it; you just do it, like brushing your teeth. This momentum is precious, because once a habit is firmly established, you can even increase intensity gradually *if* needed. But the base habit needs to be solid first. Jog for 10 minutes daily before worrying about running a marathon; write one page a day before aiming to publish a book. As an old proverb says, *"Little by little, one travels far."*

Another reason consistency triumphs is that it prevents burnout. Bob's approach of reading 70 pages in one go left him tired and reluctant to pick up the book the next day. Alice, reading a manageable amount, finished each session feeling accomplished and ready for more tomorrow. **Consistency is gentle; intensity can be harsh.** By being consistent, you make progress in a sustainable, enjoyable way, which means you're more likely to keep going and *stick with it* for the long haul. And sticking with it is the name of the game.

So, ask yourself not "How much can I do right now?" but rather "What can I do *every day* without fail?" It's far better to walk for 15 minutes every day than to exhaust yourself with a 2-hour hike once a month. It's better to meditate 5 minutes daily than to do an hour only on sporadic weekends. **Consistency asks for commitment; intensity often just feeds the ego.** Let go of the ego's desire to do something impressive only once. Embrace the quiet power of doing something *unimpressive but important* consistently. Over time, consistency becomes impressive.

If you ever doubt the impact of your small daily actions, remember the wisdom of an ancient Chinese proverb: *"A drip of water hollows out stone, not by force, but by falling often."* Your consistent efforts, as minor as they seem, are steadily hollowing out the stone of challenges and forging a new you. Keep going.

Figure 1: How consistent effort compounds over time, eventually outperforming sporadic intensity.

Shaping Identity — You Become What You Do

Our actions don't just produce external results; they also shape our sense of self. Every action, every habit, is like a vote for the type of person you want to be. Over time, those votes add up and you begin to believe certain things about your identity. The philosopher Aristotle observed this phenomenon over two thousand years ago:

"We are what we repeatedly do. Excellence, then, is not an act but a habit." — **Aristotle**

Consider what that means: **your identity is largely the sum of your daily habits**. If you repeatedly practice piano, day after day, you start to see yourself as a musician — not because you declared "I am a musician," but because your actions provided *evidence* for it. If you make a habit of running every morning, soon you internalize, "I am a runner." By contrast, if you constantly procrastinate on tasks or skip your commitments, you might start to label yourself "lazy" or "undisciplined," and sadly, you'll likely continue behaving in ways that confirm that identity. We humans love consistency between how we see ourselves and how we act, so once an identity sinks in, we tend to live up to it (for better or worse).

TOOLKIT REFERENCE *To consciously shape your identity through actions, use the "Identity-Based Habit Formation" and "Evidence Collection" exercises in Section 3 of the Practical Toolkit.*

The good news is you can **consciously craft your identity** by choosing your habits. Think about the kind of person you *want* to be. Be specific: maybe a healthy person, a creative person, a successful entrepreneur, a loving parent, a lifelong learner, a spiritually grounded person. Now ask: *what does that kind of person do each day?* A healthy person might take a walk daily and eat vegetables with each meal. A creative person might write a few pages or sketch every afternoon. A successful entrepreneur might set aside an hour each morning for strategic planning or learning new skills. A devoted parent might institute a habit of reading to their kids every night. When you identify those small daily actions, you've struck gold — because those actions, done consistently, will help you become exactly that person.

Habit expert James Clear puts it brilliantly: *"Every action you take is a vote for the type of person you wish to become."* Each time you perform your chosen habit, you are casting a vote for your new identity. No single vote will immediately transform how you see yourself, but as the votes accumulate, the evidence becomes undeniable. Do you want to be an organized person? Every time you tidy up your workspace or plan your day, you cast a vote for "I am organized." Do you want to be a kind person? Each small act of kindness, each kept promise to call your family, is a vote for "I am compassionate and reliable."

"Your daily actions are writing your biography, page by page, whether you're conscious of it or not." — Original

Alex's journey again is a perfect example. He wanted to see himself as a *disciplined, growth-oriented person*. In the beginning, every time he procrastinated or skipped out, a little voice in his head would sneer, "See, you're not really disciplined." He felt like an impostor when he tried to claim positive traits. But as Alex kept up his small daily promises — day after day, week after week — something shifted. He had strung together a month of consistent mornings and intentional actions. When he told himself, "I am becoming disciplined," he actually *believed it*, because he had proof. The inner critic grew quieter. Alex noticed he stood a bit taller and spoke with more confidence. By doing what a disciplined person does, he was *becoming* that person.

This works in reverse too: as you begin practicing a new habit, **embrace the identity from Day One**. Even if you've only gone running two days in a row, start thinking of yourself as "a runner in training" or simply "a runner." If you've decided to write a paragraph every day, you are now "a writer at heart." This isn't about being fake or boastful — it's about affirming the truth of your direction. You're not waiting to magically become disciplined in the far future; you're actively building that identity *right now*. Tell yourself,

"I keep my promises. I am disciplined. I take care of my body. I am a reader." Those statements might feel a bit awkward at first, but they reinforce your commitment. Over time, the line between your *current actions* and *future identity* blurs, and they become one and the same.

Be patient and loyal to the person you are becoming. There may be days you miss a habit or slip up — that's normal and human. Don't let it shatter your identity. If you see yourself as a runner and you miss three days of running due to illness, you're still a runner — just a runner who is taking a short rest and will be back at it tomorrow. In fact, handling these setbacks with grace (as we'll discuss soon) *strengthens* your identity because you prove that even when you stumble, you don't abandon who you are.

One word of caution: identity is powerful, but it should be rooted in *truthful actions*. Telling yourself "I am disciplined" means little if you aren't actually doing the work. That's just wishful thinking. The real magic is when your daily actions and your self-image start feeding into each other. With each promise kept, you *feel* disciplined, and feeling disciplined makes it easier to keep the next promise. It's a virtuous cycle: **action →evidence → identity → motivation → more action**. And it all starts with those initial actions. So, if you've struggled with seeing yourself positively, start with *small wins*. Prove to yourself, for yourself, that you can change. Bit by bit, rewrite the story you tell about who you are.

Reflect for a moment: *What identity do you aspire to?* And what is one small daily habit that identity would do without fail? If "I am a calm, centered person" is your desired identity, maybe your habit is five minutes of morning meditation. If "I am a proactive student" is what you want to be, maybe it's reviewing notes for 15 minutes every evening. Find that habit and start it. Each day you do it, consciously say to yourself, "This is like me. This is who I am." It may feel new, even strange, but you are literally **shaping your identity** through these actions.

In the words of an old proverb, *"You sow a habit, you reap a character."* Your habits are how you **embody** the kind of person you want to become. So choose them wisely and stick with them. Over time, you'll glance in the mirror and realize the transformation — you *are* that healthier, wiser, more disciplined person you set out to be.

TOOLKIT REFERENCE *To handle setbacks while maintaining your new identity, practice the "Identity Preservation After Lapses" and "Compassionate Restart" techniques in Section 3 of the Practical Toolkit.*

The Identity-Action-Results Cycle

Figure 2: How actions shape identity, which influences future actions, creating either a virtuous or vicious cycle.

Momentum — The Magic of Starting and Keeping Going

One of the most empowering discoveries on the road of self-improvement is that **action creates momentum**. Often, the hardest part of any task is just *starting*. Once you begin, something almost mystical happens: the next steps become easier. Momentum carries you forward like a friendly tailwind. Knowing this, you can leverage a powerful strategy on days when you feel stuck: *make the task smaller and just do the first few minutes*. If you're dreading a 30-minute workout, tell yourself, "Okay, I'll do just 5 minutes." If you're avoiding cleaning the house, commit to just "one drawer" or "picking up 5 items." If you need to study and can't bear the thought, open the book and read one page. By lowering the barrier to entry, you trick yourself into starting — and more often than not, you'll end up doing much more than you intended once you get in the flow.

Even if you truly stop after those 5 minutes, you've succeeded. Why? Because you kept your promise and you maintained momentum. You reinforced the identity of "someone who *does* something about it." And usually, you'll find that once the wheels are turning, inertia works in your favor. *An object in motion stays in motion.* Newton's first law might be about physics, but it applies wonderfully to human behavior too.

"The first step is always the heaviest—after that, momentum becomes your ally." — Original

The key is to never underestimate the power of a **single small action done right now**. As the ancient proverb says, *"The best time to plant a tree was 20 years ago. The second best time is now."* There is no benefit in waiting and wishing you had started earlier. The next best thing is to just start *today*. That first push — planting the seed, taking the step — is where momentum begins.

Of course, life isn't perfect and you will have days where despite your best efforts, you stumble. Maybe an emergency disrupts your routine, or you just genuinely feel off and skip your habit. It's important in those moments to respond in a way that preserves your momentum in the long term. **Don't let a slip turn into a slide.** If you miss one day, forgive yourself — but make sure you show up the next. A popular piece of advice is, "Never miss twice." If today broke your streak, treat tomorrow as *sacred* — a chance to right the ship.

Maintain a positive attitude towards setbacks. Instead of the harsh *"Ugh, I failed, I'm so weak,"* try a compassionate reframe: *"I missed my workout today. It's okay — it was a tough day. What can I learn from this? Maybe I scheduled it too late in the day when I'm usually tired. Tomorrow I'll do it first thing in the morning."* With this mindset, even a misstep becomes useful feedback rather than a complete derailment. **Momentum isn't about never falling; it's about always getting back up one more time.** Think of a baby learning to walk — they fall repeatedly, but each time they get up, they're a bit stronger and a bit more steady. By the hundredth fall, they're walking confidently. Your habit journey is similar. A fall is not the end; it's part of the process.

TOOLKIT REFERENCE *To build and maintain momentum, use the "Five-Minute Start Rule" and "Streak Recovery Protocol" in Section 3 of the Practical Toolkit.*

To keep momentum strong, also remember to **celebrate small wins**. Did you do your habit every day this week? Give yourself a high-five (literally, go ahead!). Treated yourself kindly when you missed a day and then got back on track? That's huge — acknowledge it. These little celebrations build a positive association with your journey. They make you feel good about progress, which fuels — you guessed it — more momentum. Success breeds success.

It can help to track your progress visually. Use a calendar or habit tracker and put a big X or checkmark on each day you complete your habit. As the days pile up, you'll see a chain of successes forming. After a week, you won't want to break the chain. After a month, that streak will be *so motivating* to continue. This is momentum you can see. If you're ever feeling low, glance at that calendar and remind yourself how far you've come, one day at a time.

Finally, make sure you're keeping your habits **enjoyable and meaningful** for you. Momentum is strongest when you're not forcing yourself out of sheer willpower, but actually finding some joy or personal reward in what you're doing. If you hate an activity, consider tweaking it: maybe jogging is miserable, but dance workouts are fun — do those instead. If journaling feels like a chore, try a voice memo diary or jotting down just one insight a day. There's always a way to align your habits with what *energizes* you. That way, once you start, it feels good to keep going.

In summary, the formula for momentum is: **start small, keep going, adjust when needed, and celebrate along the way.** One step forward, and then another. When you stumble, two steps forward again. Over time, you'll notice something astonishing — what used to require a huge effort to begin now happens almost automatically. What once felt difficult now feels natural. That is momentum at work, and it's a beautiful thing.

How Technology Can Support or Undermine Discipline

In our digital age, technology can be either your strongest ally or your greatest obstacle on the path to discipline. Here's how to leverage tech wisely:

Digital Tools That Strengthen Discipline:

- **Habit tracking apps** that provide visual progress and streaks

- **Smart device reminders** that cue you at optimal times

- **Productivity timers** like Pomodoro apps to structure focused work

- **Guided meditation or workout apps** that make it easier to start

- **Journaling apps** that prompt your reflection and make tracking growth convenient

- **Goal-sharing platforms** where you can find community and accountability

Digital Pitfalls to Avoid:

- **Notification overload** that fragments attention and depletes willpower

- **Social media comparison** that discourages your own progress

- **Endless content streams** that foster passive consumption over active growth

- **Planning apps that substitute for action** (where organizing goals becomes a form of procrastination)

- **Instant gratification** of digital rewards undermining delayed gratification skills

- **Sleep disruption** from late-night screen use affecting next-day discipline

The key is intentionality. Use technology as a servant to your discipline, not as a master. Create clear boundaries around when and how you'll engage with digital tools, ensuring they enhance rather than replace your inner compass of self-discipline.

Living It: Discipline as a Way of Life

By now, we've explored how keeping promises to yourself builds the very **core of self-discipline**, how choosing discipline over fleeting motivation leads to freedom, why slow and steady consistency outshines sporadic intensity, and how your daily habits are shaping *you* with every choice. It's time to bring all these elements together and paint a picture of what life can look like when these principles are put into practice.

Consider an ordinary person who decides to live with extraordinary discipline — perhaps someone like our friend Alex, or maybe **you**, if you choose. How might a day in the life of a disciplined person flow?

It starts with a promise kept at dawn: the alarm goes off early, and instead of bargaining for extra minutes, you remember *"If I snooze, I lose — not just time, but a bit of self-respect."* So you take a breath and rise. That simple act is a victory, filling you with a quiet confidence. By the time most people are still in bed, you've already done a few key things that align with your goals. Maybe you've hydrated and felt your body wake up with gratitude. Perhaps you've moved your body — a brisk walk or a quick stretch — getting the blood flowing and telling yourself *"Yes, I care for my health."* You might spend a few minutes in silence, meditating or planning your day, because you value a clear mind. By breakfast, you've fed both body and mind with something nourishing — a healthy meal, a few pages of a good book, or an inspiring podcast.

"A life of discipline isn't a prison of rules—it's the freedom to become your highest self with each intentional choice." — Original

Through the day, discipline shows up in little choices: you tackle the hard task at work first rather than procrastinating. When stress hits, you pause to breathe instead of react impulsively. You keep your word to your colleague or client, even if it means extra effort. And when temptation comes — to skip the gym after work or to scroll on your phone instead of playing with your kids — you recall why you started these habits. You remember the promises and the identity you're forging. So you show up for that workout, even if it's shorter today. You engage fully with your family, even if part of you is tired. And guess what? Those actions end up energizing you more than an evening of TV ever could, because they are in line with your values.

By nightfall, you take a few minutes to reflect. Maybe you journal a couple of lines: What went well today? What am I grateful for? Where did I keep my promises? Where did I slip, and what can I learn from it? This simple reflection, done with honesty and self-compassion, closes the day with awareness. If you made a mistake, you acknowledge it without harsh judgment ("I missed my reading time; I got caught up at work. Tomorrow I'll read at lunch instead."). If you achieved a win, you give yourself credit ("I was nervous about that presentation, but I prepared and it went well — proud of myself for that."). Then you plan for tomorrow: laying out workout clothes or setting a to-do priority. You go to bed not with a mind racing in regret or self-criticism, but with a sense of calm accomplishment. You kept the chain intact. You lived this day intentionally, a day true to your best self.

TOOLKIT REFERENCETo develop a framework for living disciplined daily, practice the "Morning Power Ritual" and "Evening Review Protocol" in Section 3 of the Practical Toolkit.

This might sound idealized, but it's very much attainable — not through perfection, but through consistency and course-correcting when needed. A disciplined life is not a rigid, joyless life; on the contrary, it's a life of profound satisfaction. You gain a deep sense of agency knowing "I am designing my life, not letting life just happen to me." As author Napoleon Hill famously said, "Do not wait; the time will never be 'just right.' Start where you stand, and work with whatever tools you have." You have all the tools you need to start building your disciplined life now — your next small action, your next decision, is your tool. Use it.

Before we conclude, let's turn inward one more time. Take a moment to picture your "best self" — the person you truly want to be. What does a typical day in the life of that best-you look like? What habits would that version of you be doing consistently? Now, gently compare it to your recent days. The gap between the two is not permanent; it's simply a guide pointing you to which daily habits could bridge the distance. Maybe it's waking up a bit earlier to create calm time. Maybe it's finally committing to that evening class or personal project. Maybe it's treating people (and yourself) with more patience. Whatever it is, identify one habit that would make the biggest difference, and vow to start practicing it daily.

You might even challenge yourself: try it for the next 7 days, every day, without exception. Mark each day off and see how you feel at the end of the week. Chances are you'll feel a shift — a sense of momentum and pride. If you miss a day, note why and jump back in. It's not about all-or-nothing; it's about growth. By doing this, you're not just reading about discipline — you're living it, and that makes all the difference.

Bridge to Chapter 4: From Discipline to Mindset

Just as discipline gives structure to your values, a resilient mindset gives sustainability to your discipline. Together, they form an unshakable foundation for personal growth. In the next chapter, you'll discover how to master your thoughts and emotions—the inner landscape that ultimately determines how you experience life's journey.

Remember, all the discipline in the world cannot overcome a mind filled with doubt or negativity. But when you learn to manage your inner world as skillfully as you manage your actions, you become truly unstoppable. Let's move forward to explore this crucial dimension of self-mastery.

Reflections for the Reader

- **Promise to Self:** *Think of a promise (big or small) that you've made to yourself recently but didn't keep.* How did it feel to let yourself down? What's one step you can take **today** to begin honoring that promise? Even if it's tiny — do it, and notice how keeping your word to yourself feels.

- **Discipline Check:** Recall a time you acted not because you were motivated, but because you decided to push through anyway. How did it feel afterward? Which discomfort are you willing to endure now — the brief sting of discipline or the lasting ache of regret?

- **Consistency Plan:** Identify one small action that, if done every day, would significantly improve your life in a year. Got it? Now ask, how can you make that action so easy it's almost silly *not* to do it? Design that as your daily habit and try it for one week straight.

- **Identity Shift:** Who do you want to become? Write down **I am [your desired identity]**. Under it, list three habits or behaviors that person would do daily. Tomorrow when you wake up, read that statement and commit to acting like that person, *one habit at a time.*

- **Momentum Move:** What is one task or goal you've been procrastinating on? Decide on the *smallest possible step* and do it *right after reading this chapter.* Just start — even for 2 minutes. Then give yourself credit for breaking the inertia. How does it feel to be in motion?

TOOLKIT REFERENCE *To deepen your practice of daily discipline, complete the "Weekly Discipline Challenge" and "Identity Reinforcement Letter" in Section 3 of the Practical Toolkit.*

Closing Thoughts

Discipline, habits, consistency — these aren't just self-help buzzwords. They are the quiet architects of every great life. By keeping your promises to yourself, choosing discipline over impulse, and taking steady steps each day, you are literally **building your future**. On some days, the changes may seem imperceptible, but have faith in the process. As long as you're moving forward, even inch by inch, you're on the right track.

"Your life tomorrow is being built by the quiet decisions you make today—choose wisely." — Original

Always remember why you embarked on this journey of self-improvement: because your goals and values *matter*. You *matter*. Each act of discipline is an act of self-love — it's saying "I believe I deserve to reach my dreams, so I will put in the work for them." Not every day will be easy, but every day is an opportunity to write a new line in the story of your life. Make it count.

As you close this chapter, carry this final thought with you: *In the end, the greatest promise you'll ever keep is the one you make to yourself.* Keep that promise, nurture it daily, and there is no limit to the growth and greatness you can achieve. You've got this — one day at a time, brick by brick. Your future self is already smiling back in gratitude for the work you begin today.

4

— • —

MASTERING THE INNER GAME — MIND AND EMOTIONS

"You have power over your mind — not outside events. Realize this, and you will find strength."** — *Marcus Aurelius*

Maya sat in her car in the empty parking lot long after everyone else had left, hands clenched tightly around the steering wheel. Her presentation that afternoon had gone *terribly*. Her voice cracked, she lost her train of thought, and she could sense the disapproval in her boss's eyes. Now, replaying the fiasco in her mind, Maya felt a lump rise in her throat. **"I'm such a failure,"** she whispered to herself. A flood of negative thoughts poured in: *I'll never be good at public speaking. Everyone must think I'm incompetent.* Her cheeks burned with embarrassment even in the silence of her car. She felt the sting of tears and shut her eyes, wishing she could simply disappear. This was the kind of moment that could break her spirit — and a year ago, it might have. But today, something was different.

As she sat there on the verge of tears, Maya remembered a piece of advice her grandfather had given her when she was a teenager nervous about a big exam. He had said, **"Stand guard at the door of your mind."** At the time, she didn't fully understand what he meant. But now those words came back to her. She took a shaky deep breath and tried to step back from the torrent of thoughts. Instead of *automatically* accepting **"I'm a failure"** as the truth, she questioned it. *Is one bad presentation really the end of my career?* she thought. *I had a rough day, but I've done good work before. Maybe I'm just really tired and stressed.* She sat up a little straighter, wiping her eyes. In that moment, Maya made a decision: she wouldn't let this one setback define her.

Still feeling the weight of disappointment, Maya remembered something else — a quote she had stuck on her fridge at home: **"You can't hire someone else to do your push-ups for you."** Her grandfather loved that Jim Rohn quote, reminding her that no one could do her inner work for her. If she wanted to overcome this, she had to dig deep and do the *mental push-ups* herself. So she did. Maya pulled out a crumpled notebook from her bag and started writing. She listed every self-defeating thought echoing in her mind: *I'm not cut out for this job; I always mess up when it counts; My team must think I'm useless.* Seeing these harsh thoughts on paper startled her — she would *never* say such cruel things to a friend. Gently, she began to challenge each thought. *"I always mess up"*? she wrote. *No, I've had plenty of successes, too. Today was just a bad day. "I'm not cut out for this"? Actually, I am learning skills that I've never had to use before. Everyone starts somewhere.* Line by line, Maya **reframed** the story she was telling herself. Her breathing slowed, and a sense of calm determination began to replace the despair.

TOOLKIT REFERENCE *To practice reframing negative thoughts in moments of stress, see the "Thought Challenge Protocol" and "Belief Examination Worksheet" in Section 4 of the Practical Toolkit.*

Before driving home that evening, Maya made one more conscious choice: she would treat herself with the same compassion she'd offer to a dear friend. *If my best friend had this kind of day,* she thought, *I would give her a hug and tell her one presentation doesn't erase all her hard work.* So, instead of beating herself up, Maya whispered aloud, **"It's okay. You had a rough day, but you're going to learn from this. One step at a time."** The words felt a bit awkward, but also strangely comforting. She allowed herself a warm smile — a small gesture of forgiveness and encouragement to herself.

In the weeks that followed, Maya turned her setback into a personal comeback. She began practicing short **mindfulness breaks** at work, stepping away for a few minutes to breathe whenever stress crept up. She paid closer attention to her feelings instead of bottling them in. When she felt anxious about another presentation, she acknowledged it: *I'm feeling nervous, and that's natural.* She prepared diligently, reminded herself of past successes, and even tried a quick breathing exercise right before presenting. The result? Her next presentation went **significantly better**. It wasn't perfect, but she handled questions calmly and even caught herself smiling during the process. Each challenge she faced in those weeks — even a tense client meeting that would have normally rattled her — became easier to navigate. Maya's colleagues noticed her newfound poise. One afternoon her boss even remarked, **"I can see a real change in you. You're handling pressure well these days."** Maya simply grinned, thinking of the inner work she'd been doing. She had discovered the power of mastering her mind and emotions. What had felt like a disastrous failure became, in hindsight, the turning point that made her stronger.

"The quality of your life is determined not by what happens to you, but by how you respond inside your mind to what happens." — Original

Maya's story is a testament to the **inner transformation** that's possible when we learn to master our mindset and emotions. She learned, step by step, to recognize her negative thoughts and rewrite them, to stay aware of her feelings, to be kind to herself, to find calm in chaos, and to view setbacks as lessons rather than verdicts. In essence, she built an inner toolkit that turned a painful experience into fuel for growth. *We all face moments like Maya's.* We might not all be giving work presentations, but we've all felt the sting of failure, the weight of self-doubt, or the heat of overwhelming stress. The specifics differ, but the inner challenge is the same: will you be defeated by your inner critic and turbulent emotions, or will you rise above them? The good news is, **you can learn to rise**. Just as Maya did, you can cultivate what we might call *mental mastery* — the ability to guide your thoughts and manage your emotions, even when life throws you curveballs.

In this chapter, we'll delve into how to build that mental mastery for yourself. Think of it as equipping yourself with your own emotional resilience toolkit. We'll explore five key practices for inner growth: **recognizing and reframing negative thoughts, practicing emotional awareness, building self-compassion, using mindfulness to stay calm under stress, and adopting a growth mindset.** Each of these tools will strengthen you from the inside out, so you can navigate challenges with greater ease and stay true to your goals and values even when things get tough. By the end of this chapter, you'll not only understand these concepts intellectually — you'll also have actionable techniques (and a few inspiring stories and quotes) to help you apply them in your daily life. Let's dive into your inner journey of mental mastery.

Recognize and Reframe Negative Thoughts: Rewriting Your Inner Story

Our minds are like constant storytellers, always chattering away with interpretations of what's happening. Sometimes the story is positive: *"I handled that well, I'm proud of myself."* Other times, the story is harsh: *"I always mess up. Nothing ever goes right for me."* To master your mind, you must become the **watchman at the gate of your thoughts** -- or as Jim Rohn put it, *"Stand guard at the door of your mind."* Pay attention to the narratives running through your head, especially the negative ones, because **the quality of your life is determined by the quality of your thoughts**. If you constantly tell yourself you're not good enough, you'll feel defeated and start to act that way. But if you learn to catch those negative thoughts and **reframe** them into more empowering ones, you change the entire narrative of your life.

The Thought-Feeling-Action Connection

This simple framework illustrates how our thoughts directly influence our emotions, which then drive our behaviors. By intervening at the thought level, we can transform the entire chain reaction.

Common Negative Thought Patterns. In psychology, many of those harsh, discouraging stories we tell ourselves are known as *cognitive distortions* -- basically, mental habits that twist reality like a funhouse mirror. Everyone falls into these traps sometimes. Here are a few common ones to watch out for:

- **Overgeneralizing:** You take one negative experience and draw broad, gloomy conclusions from it. For example, one bad presentation means *"I'll never succeed at this job -- I'm just terrible at speaking."* In truth, one event is just one event, not a prophecy of your whole future.

- **Catastrophizing:** The moment something goes wrong, you imagine the absolute worst-case scenario. *"I missed a deadline; now I'm sure I'll get fired and never find another job!"* This is blowing a setback way out of proportion, turning a fixable issue into an imagined disaster.

- **All-or-Nothing Thinking:** Seeing things in black-and-white extremes, with no middle ground. *"If I'm not perfect, I've failed completely. I did well on 9 tasks, but made one mistake -- so I'm a failure."* Life is rarely all or nothing; it's mostly lived in the shades of gray in between.

TOOLKIT REFERENCE *To identify your personal thought patterns, use the "Cognitive Distortion Detector" and "Mental Filter Finder" exercises in Section 4 of the Practical Toolkit.*

When thoughts like these go unchallenged, they create painful emotions and can even derail your progress. But here's the empowering truth: **a thought is not necessarily a fact**. It's just a mental event --- and you have the power to question it and change it. This realization is huge. It means that even if you can't control every situation, you *can* control how you interpret and respond to a situation by guiding your thoughts.

Reframing Your Inner Dialogue. A useful tool from psychology (specifically Cognitive Behavioral Therapy, or CBT) teaches us that our thoughts directly affect our feelings and actions. Change your thought, and you change how you feel and what you do. *Reframing* is the practice of taking a negative, distorted thought and consciously replacing it with a more realistic, constructive one. It's like editing the script of your internal movie to make sure it's encouraging rather than defeating.

60-Second Thought Reframing Exercise

When you catch yourself in a negative thought spiral, take one minute to shift your perspective:

1. **Write down the negative thought** exactly as it appears in your mind.

2. **Identify the distortion** (overgeneralizing, catastrophizing, etc.).

3. **Challenge it** with questions: "Is this 100% true? What evidence contradicts this thought?"

4. **Create a balanced alternative** that acknowledges reality but offers hope and possibility.

For example, if you think: *"I messed up that project. I'll never be successful."*

Your reframe might be: *"I made some mistakes on this project, but I've succeeded at many others. This is one setback I can learn from to improve next time."*

Try this with one of your own negative thoughts right now. Notice how differently you feel after reframing.

"Your mind will believe what you tell it. Feed it truth, not fear; possibility, not limitation; growth, not defeat." — Original

Reframing is a mental skill, and like any skill it gets stronger with practice. In the beginning, your negative thoughts might slip by unnoticed or it might be hard to come up with a positive reframe. That's okay. The key first step is **awareness**. One practical exercise to build this skill is keeping an "ANT Journal" — ANT stands for **Automatic Negative Thoughts** (those sneaky, reflex-like negative thoughts that scurry into your mind). For the next week, try this: each time you notice a self-defeating or critical thought, jot it down in a notebook or a notes app on your phone. Don't judge yourself for having it, just record it. At the end of the day, review your notes and pick one or two to **reframe** in writing. Next to each negative thought, write a kinder or more balanced alternative. If you wrote, *"I'll never get better at this,"* you might reframe it to, *"With time and practice, I can improve at this. Everyone starts somewhere."* If you catch a thought like, *"My friend hasn't texted back, they must be upset with me,"* you could reframe it as, *"They might just be busy; I'll give it some time or reach out again later."* By doing this regularly, you train yourself to *stand guard* at your mind's door, spotting negative patterns and redirecting them before they drag you down.

Reflection: Think of one recurring negative thought you've had recently. Write it down on paper or in your journal. Now ask yourself honestly: is that thought 100% true, or is it exaggerated? Challenge it. Then practice **reframing** it into a more realistic and encouraging thought. For example, if your thought was *"I'm so behind in my studies; I must be stupid,"* you might reframe it to *"I'm struggling with this subject right now, but I can seek help, manage my time better, and improve step by step."* Notice how the new thought makes you feel compared to the old one.

Every time you catch and reframe a negative thought, you're doing a mental push-up. It may not seem like much at first, but these small mental reps build **inner strength** over time. You move from being at the mercy of your thoughts to being the **director** of them. Instead of passively believing every self-criticism that pops up, you become curious and challenge their truth. This is a foundational tool in your mental mastery toolkit: *thought awareness and reframing*. Even if external events are chaotic, you can choose the meaning you give them. As the saying goes, *"Every day, stand guard at the door of your mind."* Protect your mind from unwarranted negativity and invite in thoughts that serve your growth.

TOOLKIT REFERENCE *To strengthen your reframing skills, practice the "Reframe Rehearsal" and "Evidence Gathering" exercises in Section 4 of the Practical Toolkit.*

Practice Daily Emotional Awareness: Name It to Tame It

Mastering your mindset is vital, but what about the swirling sea of **emotions** we all experience? Just like thoughts, our feelings can guide us or mislead us depending on how we handle them. Emotional mastery begins with a simple yet profound step: **awareness**. In other words, regularly noticing and naming what you feel. It might sound obvious, but many of us go through our days so busy or so conditioned to "keep it together" that we hardly acknowledge our emotional undercurrent. We might suddenly snap at someone or feel utterly exhausted and not realize those are signs of unaddressed feelings.

Why is tuning into your emotions so important? Because you **cannot change what you aren't aware of.** Feelings that are ignored or suppressed don't actually disappear -- they often just find a backdoor into your life, sometimes as stress, burnout, or unexpected bursts of anger or sadness that seem to come out of nowhere. There's a saying: *"Emotions that are buried alive never die."* They'll keep resurfacing until they're acknowledged. The solution is to routinely check in with yourself in a curious, non-judgmental way. By doing so, you shine a light on what's going on inside, and only then can you respond to it in a healthy manner.

Psychologist Daniel Goleman, who popularized the concept of Emotional Intelligence (EQ), explains that people with high EQ are adept at recognizing, understanding, and managing their own emotions. This leads to better stress management, healthier relationships, and wiser decisions. So let's start with the first part of that equation: **recognizing** your emotions. Think of it as building an internal radar for your feelings.

"Unacknowledged emotions don't disappear—they just go underground and emerge as symptoms rather than solutions." — Original

Expand Your Emotional Vocabulary

Most of us use a limited set of emotional words (happy, sad, angry, scared), but our emotional experiences are much richer and more nuanced. Having precise words to describe what you're feeling helps you understand yourself better and respond more effectively.

Instead of just "Angry," you might be feeling:

- **Irritated**: Minor annoyance or aggravation

- **Frustrated**: Blocked from a goal or outcome

- **Resentful**: Harboring bitterness about unfairness

- **Indignant**: Angry due to something unjust

- **Exasperated**: Pushed to the limit of patience

- **Enraged**: Intense, overwhelming anger

Instead of just "Sad," you might be feeling:

- **Disappointed**: Letdown about a specific outcome

- **Melancholy**: A quiet, thoughtful sadness

- **Dejected**: Discouraged and low in energy

- **Grief-stricken**: Deep sorrow from a loss

- **Lonely**: Sadness from feeling disconnected

- **Despondent**: Feeling hopeless or defeated

Instead of just "Happy," you might be feeling:

- **Content**: Peaceful satisfaction

- **Joyful**: Lively, exuberant happiness

- **Grateful**: Appreciative and thankful

- **Proud**: Pleased with an achievement

- **Optimistic**: Positive about the future

- **Inspired**: Mentally stimulated to create or act

Instead of just "Scared," you might be feeling:

- **Anxious**: Worried and uneasy

- **Nervous**: On edge, restless

- **Intimidated**: Feeling smaller or less capable

- **Insecure**: Uncertain about yourself

- **Apprehensive**: Anticipating something difficult

- **Terrified**: Intense, overwhelming fear

Try using these more specific words during your emotional check-ins. The precision helps you understand exactly what you're feeling and why.

How to Check In with Your Emotions (in 4 Steps). I encourage you to develop a habit of doing a brief emotional "check-in" once or twice a day. It can be as quick as one minute, perhaps during a lunch break and again in the evening. Here's a simple way to do it:

1. **Pause and Ask:** Literally pause whatever you're doing for a moment. Take a deep breath and ask yourself, *"What am I feeling right now?"* Turn your attention inward. Are you feeling anxious? Content? Irritated? Excited? Maybe you're feeling multiple things at once. See if you can put a name to it. Sometimes just finding the word (*"I feel overwhelmed"* or *"I feel hopeful"*) brings clarity.

2. **Acknowledge the Feeling:** Simply acknowledge that the emotion is there, without judging it as good or bad. You might even say it out loud or jot it down:

"I feel angry," or *"I feel nervous."* This might sound trivial, but in doing so, you're validating your own experience. It's like telling yourself, *"It's okay that I feel this; it's real and I'm allowed."*

3. **Explore the Why (if possible):** Next, ask yourself, *"What might be causing this feeling?"* Connect the dots if you can. Maybe you notice, *"I'm feeling anxious because I have an upcoming deadline,"* or *"I'm feeling frustrated after that meeting where my ideas weren't heard."* Understanding the source can itself be relieving -- it turns an amorphous cloud of emotion into a message you can learn from. If the cause isn't immediately clear, that's alright; sometimes emotions are cumulative or from multiple sources.

4. **Respond with Care:** Finally, ask, *"What do I need right now, given this feeling?"* This shifts you from just observing your emotion to taking a healthy action. If you're stressed, maybe you need a 5-minute break or a quick walk outside to clear your head. If you're sad, perhaps reaching out to talk with a trusted friend would help. If you're angry, you might decide to cool off before responding to whatever provoked you. The goal is to **honor** the emotion with a constructive response, rather than ignoring it or reacting impulsively.

TOOLKIT REFERENCE *To develop your emotional awareness, use the "Emotion Vocabulary Expansion" and "Body-Emotion Mapping" exercises in Section 4 of the Practical Toolkit.*

This whole check-in process can take as little as a minute or two once you get the hang of it. It's a habit of turning inward and being present with yourself. Neuroscience has a catchy phrase for one of the benefits of this practice: *"Name it to tame it."* What that means is that when you **label an emotion**, you actually reduce its intensity in the brain. If you're overwhelmed with stress, simply saying to yourself, *"I'm feeling a lot of stress right now,"* can create a small but meaningful shift. You move from *being* the emotion to *observing* the emotion. Instead of *"I am overwhelmed,"* which feels all-encompassing, it becomes *"I notice that I feel overwhelmed."* That little bit of mental distance -- seeing the emotion as an experience, not your identity -- gives you power. In that space, you can choose how to respond rather than being swept away by the feeling.

Another part of emotional awareness is expanding your **emotional vocabulary**. Often we stick to just a few labels like happy, sad, angry, or stressed. But human emotions are rich and varied. The more precisely you can identify what you're feeling, the better you can address it. For instance, "angry" might actually be *"resentful"* or *"frustrated"* or *"irritated."* "Sad" could be *"disappointed," "lonely,"* or *"grieving."* Each of those has a slightly different flavor and might call for a different response. It's like a painter having more colors on their palette -- you can paint a clearer picture of your inner experience. So, try to go beyond the basics when naming your feelings. If you notice you're "upset," dig a bit: are you *anxious* upset or *annoyed* upset? Curious exploration like this helps you understand yourself on a deeper level.

Equally important is **emotional honesty**. Give yourself permission to feel whatever you feel, without rushing to label certain emotions as "bad" or trying to shove them aside. Society sometimes teaches us that feeling sad or scared is weakness, or that we should "put on a brave face" no matter what. But true strength includes being honest with yourself. If a goal you worked hard for falls through and you feel discouraged, acknowledge it: *"I'm really discouraged and hurt by this setback."* That acknowledgment isn't self-pity; it's self-awareness. Only by accepting what's there can you begin to move through it. Ironically, allowing yourself to *fully feel* an emotion often makes it pass more quickly than if you resist it. It's like the difference between letting a wave wash over you versus trying to fight the wave -- one way, you stay grounded; the other, you get knocked off balance.

After you've acknowledged an emotion, you can then gently influence it or respond to it using the other tools we're learning. For example, once you admit *"I feel anxious about this new project,"* you can engage your mind to reframe any fearful thoughts contributing to that anxiety (*"I'm nervous, but that's because I care; I can channel this energy into preparation"*). Or you might use a mindfulness technique to calm the physical feelings of anxiety. But it starts with awareness.

Reflection: Recall a difficult situation you faced in the past week or two -- perhaps a conflict at work, a personal disagreement, or a setback in pursuing a goal. What emotions did you experience during that situation? Be as specific as you can: for example, *"hurt," "anger," "embarrassment,"* or *"fear."* Write down at least two or three. Next, consider how you *responded* to those emotions at the time. Did you react in the heat of the moment (maybe said something you regret, or shut down and withdrew)? Or did you cope in a healthy way (perhaps took some deep breaths, sip water, continue a bit of work, or just observe the urge). Finally, ask yourself: *If a similar situation happens again, what's a healthier way I could respond to those feelings?* Maybe it's pausing before you react, or expressing your feelings using "I" statements, or seeking support. By reflecting on this, you're training your emotional intelligence. You're learning to recognize your feelings and plan better responses -- so next time, you can navigate the storm with more grace.

Making daily emotional check-ins a routine is like cleaning the dashboard of your car so you can clearly see the indicators. You'll start catching the **warning lights** early -- the subtle signs of stress, frustration, or sadness -- and can address them before they snowball. You'll also become more aware of the **positive emotions** (the "green lights") that we often overlook, like moments of peace, pride, or joy. Noticing those is important too, because they remind you what's going well and what you have to be grateful for. This regular self-awareness is the second tool in your toolkit, and it sets the stage for the next key skill: treating yourself with compassion and care, especially when things go wrong.

TOOLKIT REFERENCE *To integrate emotional awareness into your daily routine, practice the "Emotion Check-in Schedule" and "Emotion-Action Planning" exercises in Section 4 of the Practical Toolkit.*

Build Self-Compassion: Your Inner Ally in Tough Times

Now that you're becoming more mindful of your thoughts and feelings, let's talk about how you **treat yourself** during moments of struggle. This tool is perhaps the heart of emotional resilience: **self-compassion**. In simple terms, self-compassion means extending the same kindness and understanding to yourself that you would to a close friend. It sounds straightforward, yet many of us find it surprisingly difficult. Ask yourself: *When I fail or hit a setback, what does my inner voice sound like?* For a lot of people, that inner voice can be shockingly harsh. We say things to ourselves in disappointment that we would *never* say to someone we love. If a dear friend or your child came to you after a failure, you might say, *"It's okay, you gave it your best shot. Don't be too hard on yourself; you'll bounce back."* But when we look in the mirror after a failure, we might think, *"Ugh, I'm so stupid. I always ruin everything. I'm a failure."* We essentially kick ourselves when we're down.

It's time to change that. **Self-compassion** is not about making excuses or letting yourself off the hook from responsibility. In fact, it's the opposite of complacency -- it's a powerful motivator for improvement. Dr. Kristin Neff, a leading researcher on self-compassion, describes it as having three components: (1) **Mindfulness** -- acknowledging your pain without exaggeration or avoidance, (2) **Kindness** -- speaking to yourself in a caring way instead of a critical way, and (3) **Common Humanity** -- remembering that you're not alone, that being imperfect and making mistakes is a shared human experience. When you practice these, you create a supportive inner environment that actually *helps* you grow and do better. Interestingly, research shows that people who practice self-compassion tend to experience less anxiety and depression, greater resilience in the face of challenges, and even more motivation to achieve their goals. It turns out that when you encourage yourself with compassion, you're more likely to *try again* after a failure, whereas brutal self-criticism often leads to fear of failing and giving up. Think about that -- being kind to yourself when you fail makes you **more likely** to succeed in the long run, not less. It's a myth that you have to be your own drill sergeant; being your own best friend is far more effective.

"Treating yourself with compassion isn't weakness—it's the strength to be gentle with yourself when life is harsh enough already." — Original

So how do we actually build self-compassion, especially if we're used to that inner critic running the show? It starts with **mindfulness of your self-talk**. Begin to notice when that critical voice kicks in. Let's say you planned to exercise every day this week, but you missed two days. What does the voice in your head say? Maybe something like, *"See? You have no discipline. You blew it again."* As soon as you notice that, pause and **catch** those thoughts. This is where you can bring back the reframing skill you learned earlier, but now apply it to your self-talk. Ask yourself: *If my best friend were in this exact situation, feeling bad about missing some workouts, what would I say to them?* You probably wouldn't say, *"Wow, you're hopeless."* More likely, you'd gently say, *"Hey, it's okay. You missed a couple days, but look, you made it three days this week! That's a start. And even if you slipped, you can always start fresh tomorrow. Don't give up -- you're making progress."* Now, say **that** to yourself. You might literally speak it out loud or write it down: *"I'm not a failure for missing a couple of days. I've made progress, and I can continue. One setback doesn't erase my effort."* By consciously **rewriting the script** of your inner dialogue, you start to replace the inner bully with an inner coach.

TOOLKIT REFERENCE *To cultivate greater self-compassion, practice the "Self-Compassion Letter" and "Inner Critic Dialogue" exercises in Section 4 of the Practical Toolkit.*

Two-Minute Self-Compassion Practice

When you're feeling down on yourself, try this quick exercise:

1. **Place a hand on your heart** or another soothing touch (like hugging yourself). This physical gesture activates your body's caregiving response.

2. **Acknowledge your difficulty**: "This is a moment of suffering" or "I'm having a hard time right now."

3. **Connect with our shared humanity**: "Everyone struggles sometimes; I'm not alone in feeling this way."

4. **Offer yourself kindness**: "May I be kind to myself in this moment. I'm doing the best I can."

Try this now with something that's been troubling you. Notice how it feels to treat yourself with genuine care rather than criticism.

Sometimes it helps to formalize this process with an exercise called the **Self-Compassion Letter**. It might feel a bit awkward at first, but it's incredibly powerful. When you're really beating yourself up -- say you got a poor result on something important or you're feeling shame about a mistake -- take 10 minutes to write a letter *to yourself* from the perspective of a wise, compassionate friend or mentor. In this letter, acknowledge your feelings and struggles. For example: *"Dear Me, I know you're feeling really down and disappointed that you didn't pass that exam. It's understandable -- you worked hard and it hurts to fall short."* Validate what you're going through. Then offer words of kindness and encouragement: *"But please remember, this one exam doesn't define you. Everyone stumbles sometimes -- it's part of being human and learning. I believe in you. I've seen how dedicated you are. Take some time to rest and then consider what you might do differently next time. You've got this."* Write in a tone that's supportive and loving. The first time you try this, you might be surprised at how much of a difference it makes. Many people (myself included) find that after writing such a letter, their mood shifts from despair to hope. Nothing externally has changed -- the only difference is **your attitude toward yourself**. You trade self-judgment for self-encouragement.

Another self-compassion technique you can try on the spot is a short **self-compassion meditation** or mantra. You don't have to be a meditation expert. Simply sit quietly for a minute or two, maybe place a hand on your heart (a gesture of comfort to yourself), and repeat a gentle phrase in your mind. Something like: *"May I be kind to myself in this moment. May I find peace and strength."* Choose words that feel natural and soothing to you. You can close your eyes and breathe slowly as you say them. It might sound a bit "fluffy," but it's effectively giving yourself the reassurance that we all crave in tough times. Think of it as administering first aid to an emotional wound. If you notice you're drowning in self-criticism, pause and try this kind of compassionate breathing or say a kind phrase to yourself. It's the antidote to the poison of that harsh inner voice.

A **huge** part of self-compassion is also remembering that **you're not alone** in your struggle. This is the "common humanity" piece. When we fail or feel inadequate, we often fall into the trap of *isolating* ourselves mentally: *"It's just me. Everyone else is doing fine; I'm the only one who screws up like this."* But that's an illusion. *Every single person* you admire or think has it all together has faced failure, disappointment, and moments of doubt. All of us are imperfect; all of us are works in progress. When you make a mistake or fall short, remind yourself of this truth: *"Everyone messes up sometimes. This feeling of failure is something anyone would feel in my shoes. I'm not alone, and this doesn't mean I'm broken --- it means I'm human."* This perspective can really lighten the burden. It transforms shame (which is *"I'm bad"* and isolates you) into empathy (which is *"this is tough, but others go through it too, and we can all overcome"*). For instance, if you lost your temper and yelled at your kids one evening, instead of sinking into *I'm a terrible parent*, you can remind yourself: *"Parenting is hard. Everyone loses patience sometimes. What matters is that I recognize it, apologize, and try to do better. I'm learning just like every other parent."* By viewing your experience as part of the larger human experience, you escape that lonely corner your inner critic tried to trap you in.

Reflection: Think of a recent failure or setback that really hurt you -- something that made you feel disappointed in yourself. Maybe you didn't get a job you interviewed for, or you slipped back into an old habit you were trying to break, or you let someone down. First, write down a few of the actual thoughts or phrases your inner critic said to you about this event. Be honest (even if it's harsh): perhaps it was something like *"I can't do anything right,"* or *"I'm just not cut out for this,"* or *"I blew it, and everyone will think less of me."* Next, take a deep breath and imagine that instead of *you*, it was your closest friend who experienced this exact setback and now they're confiding in you, feeling exactly how you felt. What would you genuinely say to comfort and encourage them? Write that down, addressing it to yourself by name. Maybe something like, *"Hey_____, I know you're really hurting over this. I want you to remember that this one setback doesn't erase all the good things you've done. You tried your best, and that matters. And just because it didn't work out this time doesn't mean you won't succeed in the future. Every success story has chapters of failure and learning. You are capable and worthy, no matter what. Give yourself some time to recover, and know that I believe in you."* Now compare the two sets of messages -- the critical ones and the compassionate ones. Notice which voice feels more constructive and truthful. Keep that compassionate letter or note to yourself. The next time your inner critic starts ranting, read those kinder words and let them remind you how you *truly* want to treat yourself.

Building self-compassion is like strengthening a muscle that helps you bounce back from life's punches. When you cultivate this mindset, failures and mistakes don't crush you the way they used to. Instead of your motivation and self-esteem crumbling when you slip up, they actually become more resilient. You start seeing setbacks as setups for a comeback, because you're focused on learning and encouraging yourself rather than drowning in shame. When you treat yourself with respect and care, you create an inner environment where growth and improvement flourish. Keep in mind, being good to yourself is **not selfish** or indulgent -- it actually fuels you to be stronger and more effective in everything you do, and it enables you to be more present and compassionate toward others as well. Self-compassion is the backbone of lasting resilience. By becoming your own ally, you ensure that when life gets tough, you have someone in your corner 24/7 -- *yourself*. And that makes all the difference as you face challenges with grace and grit.

Use Mindfulness to Find Calm in the Storm

Even as we work on our thoughts and practice self-compassion, life will still throw stress and emotional turbulence our way. Challenges at work, conflicts in relationships, unexpected setbacks -- these are part of the human experience. This is where **mindfulness and stress-regulation techniques** come in, the next set of tools for mental mastery. If self-compassion is like being your own best friend, mindfulness is like being your own wise, calm center in the storm. It's the practice of staying **present** and fully experiencing the moment as it is, without getting carried away by it or judging it. Think of mindfulness as a way to hit the *pause* button on life when things start to feel overwhelming, so you can regain clarity and control.

What exactly is **mindfulness**? Simply put, it means paying attention to the **here and now** on purpose and without judgment. A classic analogy is to imagine your mind as a vast sky and your thoughts and emotions as clouds passing through. Mindfulness is observing those clouds come and go without chasing after them or fighting them. For instance, if a cloud of anxiety or anger floats in, instead of immediately reacting or panicking because it's there, you just note it: *"Oh, there's anxiety"* or *"there's anger."* You allow it to be for a moment without letting it sweep you up into a storm. By doing so, you create a space to decide how to respond. In practical terms, mindfulness can be as simple as taking a conscious, deep breath and bringing your attention fully to that moment.

"Between stimulus and response lies a space of conscious choice—mindfulness helps you find and expand that space." — Original

The S.T.O.P. Method for Workplace Stress

When you feel overwhelmed at work, this 90-second mindfulness technique can help you regain your center:

1. **S - Stop** what you're doing. Pause your typing, set down your phone, close your laptop.

2. **T - Take** a breath. Breathe deeply, feeling your abdomen expand and contract.

3. **O - Observe** what's happening inside you. Notice physical sensations, emotions, and thoughts without judgment.

4. **P - Proceed** mindfully, with awareness of what you really need right now.

This technique is especially powerful in high-stakes workplace situations. Use it before important meetings, when receiving criticism, or when feeling overwhelmed by deadlines. The brief pause creates space for a wiser response rather than a knee-jerk reaction.

One of the most accessible mindfulness tools is your **breath** -- it's like a built-in stress relief remote that you carry everywhere. When you notice yourself getting anxious or angry, your heart might start racing, your muscles tense up, your thoughts spiral. That's your body's fight-or-flight response kicking in. In those moments, try this *grounding* technique: **take a slow, deep breath in** through your nose to a count of 4, feeling your belly expand as you fill your lungs... then **exhale slowly** through your mouth to a count of 6 or 7, letting your shoulders drop as you empty your lungs. Repeat this a few times. This type of breathing (longer exhale than inhale) sends a signal to your nervous system that it's okay to calm down. Almost like magic, your heart rate will start to slow and your mind will begin to clear. You can use this anytime -- before an exam or big meeting, when you're stuck in traffic and feeling frustrated, or whenever you catch yourself teetering on the edge of overwhelm. It's simple but incredibly effective. Even just **three slow breaths** can shift you from a reactive state to a more centered one.

TOOLKIT REFERENCE *To practice mindfulness in everyday situations, use the "Five Senses Grounding" and "Mindful Breathing Reset" exercises in Section 4 of the Practical Toolkit.*

Another practical technique is taking **"mindful micro-breaks."** These are tiny pockets of mindfulness sprinkled throughout your day. You don't need a meditation cushion or an hour of silence; even 30 seconds will do. Here's how: a couple of times a day, deliberately pause what you're doing and tune into the present moment. For example, you might stop at your desk, close your eyes for 15-30 seconds, and focus on the sounds around you or the feeling of your breath. If you're walking between meetings or classes, you could do a walking micro-break -- feel the contact of your feet with the ground, notice the breeze on your skin or the sensation of movement in your legs. If you're drinking water or having coffee, take one sip mindfully -- really feel the cup in your hand, the warmth or coolness, the taste as you swallow. These small acts of mindfulness act like a reset button. They pull you out of autopilot and any building stress, and anchor you in the **now**. As you do this, you might notice tension in your shoulders or jaw that you can consciously relax. You might realize your mind was racing about something that hasn't even happened yet, and gently bring your focus back to the present, where things are actually okay. Such micro-breaks prevent stress from accumulating unchecked. It's like taking pressure out of a valve periodically so you don't explode later.

Real-Life Mindfulness Success Stories

The Surgeon's Pre-Operation Ritual Dr. James Carson, a heart surgeon with a reputation for exceptional calm during high-stress procedures, credits a simple 60-second mindfulness practice before each operation. "Before I scrub in, I take one minute to breathe and center myself," he explains. "I focus completely on my breath and set an intention for the surgery."

This brief mindfulness practice has measurably improved his performance. During one particularly challenging emergency procedure where a patient's aorta ruptured un- expectedly, the operating room erupted in panic. Dr. Carson immediately employed his breathing technique, which not only steadied his own hands but had a calming effect on his team. "Mindfulness doesn't eliminate the emergency," he says, "but it creates a space where I can respond with clarity instead of react with fear." The patient survived what would typically be a fatal complication.

The Executive's Meeting Strategy Sarah Thompson, a CEO of a tech startup, trans- formed her leadership approach by implementing the S.T.O.P. method before difficult conversations. Previously known for her reactive management style, Sarah would often interrupt team members and make snap judgments during meetings.

"I was always in problem-solving mode, never truly listening," she admits. After learn- ing mindfulness techniques, she began taking 30 seconds to center herself before each meeting, and would use the S.T.O.P. method whenever she felt her impatience rising. The results were remarkable: employee satisfaction scores increased by 40% within six months, and team members reported feeling "truly heard" for the first time.

"In one particularly tense negotiation with investors, I felt myself becoming defensive as they questioned our financial projections," Sarah recalls. "Instead of responding immediately, I took a deep breath, noted my defensiveness, and asked a clarifying question instead. That pause completely changed the dynamic of the meeting—we ended up finding a solution that worked for everyone."

These real examples demonstrate how mindfulness doesn't just feel good—it creates tangible improvements in performance, relationships, and outcomes in high-pressure situations.

A tip to make sure you remember to take these breaks is to use triggers or reminders. You could set a silent alarm on your phone a couple of times a day labeled "Pause" or "Breathe." When it goes off, that's your cue to take a one-minute mindfulness break. Or you can link mindfulness to routine activities -- for instance, decide that every time you step into your car, you'll take one deep breath before turning on the engine, or each time you finish a task at work, you'll do a quick stretch and breath. These small habits weave calm moments into your day. They might seem trivial, but they are powerful in keeping your stress levels in check. Instead of letting tension snowball all day, you're actively managing it in little chunks.

Beyond these mini-breaks, you might consider a slightly longer **mindfulness practice** in your day, like a short meditation in the morning or before bed. Even 5 minutes of sitting quietly can make a difference. You don't have to "clear your mind" (a common misconception about meditation); you just gently focus on something like your breathing, a simple phrase, or sensations in your body. When (not if) your mind wanders, as it inevitably will, you simply notice it and kindly guide your attention back to your breath or focal point. Think of it like a bicep curl for your brain -- each time you notice your mind wandering and bring it back, you're strengthening your attention muscle and your ability to return to center. Over time, this can translate to daily life: you become less reactive because you've practiced catching yourself and choosing where to focus.

One beautiful mindfulness meditation that ties together mindfulness and compassion is the **Loving-Kindness Meditation** (also called *Metta* meditation). In this practice, you generate feelings of goodwill and warmth towards yourself and others. A simple way to start is by focusing on yourself. Close your eyes and silently repeat a few kind phrases directed at *you*. For example: **"May I be safe. May I be peaceful. May I be** kind to myself. May I be strong." Say these slowly in your mind, and really feel the intention behind each one. You're planting seeds of kindness in your own mind. Research has shown that this practice can increase positive emotions and reduce self-criticism. Essentially, you're cultivating emotional resilience in a meditative form -- you're training your heart and mind to default to compassion and calm.

TOOLKIT REFERENCE *To develop a deeper mindfulness practice, explore the "Loving-Kindness Meditation" and "Mindful Movement Sequence" in Section 4 of the Practical Toolkit.*

Now, mindfulness isn't just something to practice in *calm* moments; it's perhaps most useful in the **heat of the moment** -- when you find yourself in a stressful or emotionally charged situation. Let's say you're in a meeting and a coworker unexpectedly criticizes your work in front of others. You feel a surge of anger and embarrassment. In that exact moment, mindfulness is your friend. Instead of instantly reacting (maybe snapping back defensively, which you might regret later, or shutting down in shame), you *internally* take a deep breath. You notice the physical signs: *"My face is getting hot, my heart is pounding. I'm feeling anger and hurt."* Just acknowledging that to yourself is an act of mindfulness -- you're observing your inner experience. You remind yourself to *pause*. You could even excuse yourself for a minute if that's possible, just to regroup. By doing this, you give yourself a bit of space to decide the **wise response**. Mindfulness won't necessarily make the anger vanish immediately, but it will keep you from being *controlled* by that anger. You might decide, *"Okay, I'm going to address that criticism calmly, without lashing out."* Or maybe you choose to wait until after the meeting and discuss it privately when you're cooler. The key is that, by being aware, you created a **gap between the stimulus and your response**. In that gap lies your freedom to choose. Viktor Frankl, a psychiatrist and Holocaust survivor, expressed this beautifully:

"Between stimulus and response there is a space. In our response lies our growth and our freedom." --- *Viktor Frankl*

Mindfulness helps you find that space in everyday life. It puts a bit of breathing room between what happens *to* you and what you do next. And in that breathing room, you can choose a response that aligns with your values and long-term goals, rather than just reacting on impulse.

Reflection: Think of a time recently when you felt really stressed, overwhelmed, or on the verge of losing your cool. In hindsight, try to identify what physical and mental signs told you that you were in a high-stress moment. Did your shoulders tense up? Heart race?

Mind start throwing worst-case scenarios at you? Jot down a few signs you recognize. Now, brainstorm one mindfulness or calming technique you *could* have used in that moment if you had been aware. For example: *"When I felt my anger rising during that argument, I could have stepped away for five minutes to breathe."* Or *"When I was anxious about that phone call, I could have done the 4-6 breathing to calm down."* Visualize yourself doing that next time a similar situation comes up -- see yourself taking the deep breath, or consciously relaxing your body, or grounding yourself by noticing the environment. By mentally rehearsing this, you're more likely to remember to use these tools when stress flares up again.

Incorporating mindfulness and stress-regulation techniques into your daily routine might be one of the greatest gifts you give yourself. It doesn't require a huge time commitment -- just consistency and a willingness to pause. Over weeks and months of practicing, you'll likely notice you're not as easily thrown off balance by surprises or setbacks. You recover your equilibrium faster. Others might even comment that you seem calmer or more patient. That's because you're developing an **inner stability** -- a calm center that isn't so easily swayed by external chaos. It's like building a kind of superpower: the ability to maintain your cool under pressure. This superpower amplifies all the other inner skills you're working on. When you're calm and present, it's much easier to catch negative thoughts and reframe them (because your mind isn't racing). It's easier to be compassionate with yourself and others. It's easier to stick with challenges. Mindfulness, in many ways, is the foundation that allows you to *use* your other tools effectively, rather than getting hijacked by stress or emotion. With a bit of calm in your mind, you can face whatever comes with clarity and courage.

Embrace a Growth Mindset: Turning Setbacks into Stepping Stones

The final piece of our mental mastery toolkit is adopting a **growth mindset**. This concept, pioneered by psychologist Carol Dweck, is all about how we view our abilities and challenges. In a nutshell, having a growth mindset means you believe that your skills and intelligence can be **developed** over time with effort, good strategies, and help from others. The opposite is a **fixed mindset** -- the belief that your qualities are carved in stone, that you're either "good" or "bad" at something and that's just how it is. Why does this distinction matter for mastering your mind and emotions? Because if you have a growth mindset, failures and setbacks don't reflect some permanent flaw in you --- instead, they're seen as *valuable feedback* and opportunities to grow. In other words, a growth mindset makes you emotionally resilient by changing how you interpret the hard times.

Imagine two students, Alice and Ben, who both receive a poor grade on an important test. Alice has more of a fixed mindset: she thinks, *"I'm just bad at this subject. I'm not a math person (or a science person, etc.). There's no point in trying harder because this is just who I am."* She feels ashamed and might even give up or avoid that subject in the future. Ben, on the other hand, has a growth mindset. His reaction is different: *"I didn't do well yet. Looks like I need to change how I'm studying. Maybe I didn't truly understand chapters 3 and 4; I can go back and review or ask the teacher for help. I bet I can improve by the next test."* Both students feel disappointed, maybe even upset, about the grade -- that's natural. But their **mindsets** lead them down very different paths: Alice's mindset leads her to retreat and lose confidence, while Ben's mindset pushes him to adapt and try again. Over time, who do you think will perform better and feel more confident? Likely Ben, because he'll keep improving rather than shutting down.

"Every 'failure' is just feedback in disguise, showing you what to adjust on your path to growth." — Original

Sara Blakely: A Growth Mindset Success Story

Sara Blakely, the founder of Spanx and self-made billionaire, attributes much of her success to the growth mindset her father instilled in her from childhood. Every week at dinner, her father would ask her and her brother, "What did you fail at this week?" If they had nothing to report, he would be disappointed.

This unusual parenting approach taught Blakely to redefine failure. Instead of seeing it as something shameful, she saw it as evidence that she was pushing herself beyond her comfort zone and learning. She says this mindset gave her the courage to persist when starting Spanx, despite facing countless rejections and obstacles.

When manufacturers told her that her hosiery idea wouldn't work, she didn't interpret their rejection as proof of her inadequacy (fixed mindset). Instead, she saw it as information that helped her refine her approach (growth mindset). She kept seeking until she found someone willing to try her idea.

Blakely's growth mindset allowed her to:

- View setbacks as temporary rather than permanent

- Focus on learning from criticism rather than taking it personally

- Find lessons in every rejection

- See effort as the path to mastery, not something to be avoided

Her story demonstrates how a growth mindset isn't just positive thinking—it's a practical approach to challenges that leads to real-world success.

At its core, a growth mindset lets you treat setbacks as **feedback** rather than evidence of failure. Every time something doesn't go as you hoped, you can ask, *"What can I learn from this? How can I use this experience to come back stronger or smarter?"* History is full of examples of great accomplishments built on a foundation of setbacks. Thomas Edison, the inventor of the lightbulb, famously said after many experiments that didn't work, **"I have not failed. I've just found 10,000 ways that won't work."** Each "failed" experiment wasn't a verdict on his ability; it was simply information -- one more way *not* to make a lightbulb -- which brought him closer to the way that *would* work. That's growth mindset in action. You don't have to be an inventor to apply this. Let's say you applied for a job or a college and didn't get in. A fixed mindset might whisper, *"I'm not good enough; I got rejected, so why bother trying in this field again?"* But a growth mindset would respond, *"Okay, that didn't pan out this time. Maybe I need to strengthen my resume or improve my interview skills. What can I do to improve for the next opportunity? This rejection isn't a 'no' forever -- it might just be a 'not yet.'"* See how that perspective turns a dead-end into a detour towards improvement?

TOOLKIT REFERENCE *To cultivate a growth mindset, practice the "Failure Re-framing" and "Learning Opportunity Identification" exercises in Section 4 of the Practical Toolkit.*

When you adopt this way of thinking, the **sting of failure transforms into determination.** It doesn't mean failure stops hurting entirely -- it's normal to feel disappointment or frustration. But beneath those emotions, there's a steady belief: *"This is not the end of my story. I can grow from this."* That belief acts like an emotional cushion. It softens the blow and bounces you back up more quickly. You don't tie your identity or self-worth to one outcome because you see yourself as a work in progress. Any criticism or setback is just data you can use to refine that work.

Another aspect of the growth mindset is that you start to **embrace challenges** instead of avoiding them. Think of someone who avoids difficult tasks or challenges because they hate struggling or risking failure -- that's a fixed mindset at play, driven by a fear of not looking smart or capable. Now think of someone who **seeks out** tough challenges -- like a gamer who plays on a harder mode for the thrill, or an athlete who competes with slightly better players to improve their game. That's the spirit of growth. As motivational speaker Jim Rohn wisely said, *"Don't wish it was easier, wish you were better. Don't wish for fewer* *problems, wish for more skills. Don't wish for less challenge, wish for more wisdom."* Let that sink in. Instead of hoping that life will not challenge you, hope that each challenge makes you wiser and stronger. With a growth mindset, you start to see life a bit like a training ground rather than a minefield. Each obstacle isn't just something to get past; it's an occasion to develop your skill set or deepen your understanding. So when a challenge comes, you can say, *"Alright, game on -- this will teach me something."* Suddenly, even difficulties have a purpose.

Criticism, too, is handled differently with a growth mindset. None of us *enjoy* being criticized, especially if it's delivered harshly. A fixed mindset tends to take criticism personally and defensively: *"They said my presentation was weak -> they're saying I'm bad -> I feel awful and I just want to avoid any more criticism."* A growth mindset, while not *enjoying* it, will try to find the nugget of **useful feedback** in the critique: *"Okay, my manager said my time management was poor on that project. Instead of labeling myself 'terrible at time management,' I'll acknowledge there's room to improve. Maybe I can adopt a new scheduling tool or prioritize tasks differently. What can I learn from this comment?"* In this way, even criticism becomes fuel for growth rather than a dagger to the heart. You sift out what's constructive (perhaps the manager had a point about planning ahead) and discard any unnecessary negativity (maybe their tone was rude -- that part you don't need to internalize). This approach keeps your **emotional balance** -- you don't spiral into shame, because you're too busy turning the experience into a plan for self-improvement.

Having a growth mindset also nurtures **optimism** and hope. When you truly believe that you can improve and that today's failure isn't forever, it's easier to remain hopeful in tough times. Hope becomes a kind of resilience. Instead of, *"This is awful, I'll never recover,"* you think, *"This is tough right now, but I'll find a way through. I can handle this or I can learn to handle this."* This isn't about blind positivity or denying problems. You still see the problem clearly, and you still feel the disappointment or frustration. But you also see *yourself* clearly -- as someone capable of growth. Because of that, you carry an underlying confidence that, in time, things can change and you can influence that change. It's a steady voice in your mind that says, *"Keep going, you're getting better, you'll figure it out."*

TOOLKIT REFERENCE *To strengthen your ability to persevere through setbacks, try the "Growth Story Journaling" and "Not Yet Reframing" techniques in Section 4 of the Practical Toolkit.*

Chances are, you already have areas in your life where you naturally use a growth mindset. Think of a skill you're good at today that you *didn't* used to be good at. Driving a car, cooking a decent meal, playing an instrument, even using a smartphone -- anything. At one point, you were a complete novice. And you probably made mistakes (burnt food, fender-benders, wrong notes, accidentally deleted files -- whatever). But you didn't conclude, *"I failed at boiling pasta once, so I'll never cook again."* You persisted and improved. As children, we *all* had a growth mindset in many ways: we fell hundreds of times learning to walk, babbled nonsense before forming words, drew terrible crayon pictures yet kept drawing... We were **naturally resilient** learners. We didn't think, *"I fell down; I guess I'm not meant to walk."* We just kept trying until we got it. Reconnecting with that innate drive to learn and grow can transform how you approach challenges as an adult. Every stumble becomes just that -- a stumble, not the end of the road.

Reflection: Identify one area of your life where you suspect you've been holding a **fixed mindset**. Maybe you've caught yourself thinking, *"I'm just not good at ___,"* or *"I'll never be able to ___."* Write down one such belief. Now challenge that thought: What if that ability isn't set in stone? What's one small step or practice that could help you improve even slightly in that area? (For example, if you think "I'm not good at public speaking," a step might be "Volunteer to speak up in the next team meeting once" or "Practice a short speech in front of a mirror." If you think "I'm terrible at drawing," maybe "Follow a simple drawing tutorial on YouTube for beginners.") Next, recall a past setback that initially felt like a serious failure or disappointment. With time and perspective, were you able to find *any* positive outcome or lesson from it? Perhaps not getting one job led you to a different, better opportunity later, or a failed business taught you skills that helped you succeed in a new venture. Write down at least one **lesson or silver lining** from that past experience. Keep these notes as a reminder that abilities can grow and that failures often carry seeds of something beneficial.

Now, adopting a growth mindset is not a one-time switch; it's a lifelong journey of shifting your perspective when needed. Even if you generally have a growth mindset, certain areas of your life might trigger fixed thinking (we all have our sensitive spots). The key is to start *noticing* those moments and intentionally reframing them. The more you do this, the more it will become second nature. Embracing a growth mindset will supercharge your personal development. You'll start to meet challenges with a "bring it on" attitude, because deep down you know: *this is going to make me better.* Challenges become less threatening because you're not measuring your worth by success or failure;

you're focused on what you're gaining from the process. Criticism loses its sting because it doesn't define you -- it merely informs you. And failure? It stops being a finale and becomes more of a plot twist in your ongoing story of growth. As the old saying goes, you begin to see every stumbling block as a **stepping stone**. With this mindset, you become *virtually unstoppable* in pursuit of your goals. Every time you get knocked down, you don't just get back up -- you get up a bit **stronger and wiser** than before.

Conclusion: Your Emotional Resilience Toolkit in Action

We've covered a lot of ground in this chapter -- from mastering your self-talk to managing your feelings and viewing setbacks in a whole new light. Take a moment to appreciate the tools you've added to your **inner toolkit**:

- **Thought Reframing:** Catching negative thoughts and flipping them into more constructive, realistic ones. You've learned that you don't have to believe everything you think -- you can challenge and change the stories in your head.

- **Emotional Check-Ins:** Regularly naming and understanding your feelings. Remember, *"name it to tame it."* By identifying your emotions, you gain power over them instead of being powerlessly driven by them.

- **Self-Compassion:** Being kind and forgiving to yourself in moments of failure or pain -- just as you would be to a dear friend. Rather than condemning yourself, you encourage yourself, which boosts your resilience and motivation.

- **Mindfulness & Stress Relief:** Using techniques like mindful breathing, pauses throughout the day, and present-moment awareness to stay calm and centered under pressure. These practices help you respond thoughtfully to challenges instead of reacting blindly.

- **Growth Mindset:** Embracing challenges and failures as opportunities to learn, and believing in your capacity to improve. With this outlook, every setback is temporary and every effort you make contributes to your growth.

These aren't just abstract concepts -- they are **practical tools**. And like any tools, they only work if you *use* them. Now that you've gathered them, the next step is to put them into practice in your daily life. I encourage you to take a proactive approach: choose one or two tools from the list that really resonated with you, and **commit to practicing them this week**.

TOOLKIT REFERENCE *To integrate these mental mastery tools into your daily life, use the "Daily Resilience Practice Plan" and "Emotional Tool Selection Guide" in Section 4 of the Practical Toolkit.*

Emergency Mental First Aid Kit

For those moments when emotions feel overwhelming, here's a quick reference guide you can use anywhere:

When anxiety hits:

- Take 5 slow breaths (4 count in, 6 count out)

- Name what you're feeling: "This is anxiety"

- Ground yourself by naming 5 things you can see

When anger surges:

- Step away if possible, even for 30 seconds

- Place your hand on your heart and breathe

- Ask: "What's beneath this anger?"

When self-criticism attacks:

- Notice the harsh voice: "There's my inner critic"

- Ask: "Would I say this to a friend?"

- Say one kind thing to yourself

Keep this mini-toolkit in mind for life's storms. These quick interventions take less than a minute but can prevent hours of emotional suffering.

For example, you might decide to start an **ANT Journal** in a notebook -- writing down one Automatic Negative Thought each day and practicing reframing it into a positive alternative. Or you might set a daily alarm on your phone for a **midday mindfulness break** -- when it rings, you'll take 3 deep breaths and do a quick emotional check-in. Perhaps you'll try writing a short **self-compassion letter** to yourself after your next mistake or tough day, to remind you to be kind to yourself. You could make it a nightly habit to jot down **one thing you appreciated about yourself** or did well each day, to foster a kinder inner voice. Maybe there's a situation bothering you right now -- you could take ten minutes tonight to journal about it and find a **growth lesson** in it, asking, "What is this teaching me? How could this challenge make me better?" Any of these actions are ways to start using your new toolkit.

Feel free to get creative and tailor the practice to your life. The key is consistency. Just as doing one workout won't magically make you fit, using these mental and emotional exercises once won't drastically change things -- but using them consistently over time will absolutely strengthen you from the inside out. Remember Jim Rohn's analogy: *no one else can do your push-ups for you*. You have to do these inner exercises yourself, but the reward is that **you grow stronger and more resilient with each rep**.

"Inner strength isn't built in moments of ease, but in the quiet practice of mastering your responses when life tests you." — Original

Like Maya, I've had to learn these skills through my own struggles. Years ago, I faced a major professional setback that shook my confidence to the core. I found myself spiraling in self-doubt and criticism far harsher than I would ever direct at anyone else. What turned things around wasn't pretending everything was fine, but applying the very tools we've discussed in this chapter.

I began the practice of catching my catastrophic thoughts ("My career is over") and questioning their validity. I started naming my emotions as they arose instead of trying to suppress them. I learned to speak to myself with the same compassion I would offer a friend facing a similar situation. These weren't instant fixes, but daily practices that gradually changed how I experienced challenges.

What surprised me most was how these inner skills transformed my outer results. With a calmer mind and greater emotional balance, I found creative solutions I might have missed while panicking. I built stronger professional relationships because I wasn't defensive or reactive. And perhaps most importantly, I discovered a wellspring of resilience that has served me through every challenge since.

The tools in this chapter aren't just nice theories—they're battle-tested methods that can transform your relationship with yourself and with life's inevitable setbacks. Start using them today, and watch as your inner world becomes a source of strength rather than stress.

Which Tool Should You Start With? A Quick Self-Assessment

Everyone has different needs when it comes to emotional resilience. Take this quick assessment to identify which mental mastery tool might benefit you most right now:

1. **What's your biggest emotional challenge lately?**

   ○ Constantly criticizing yourself → Start with **Self-Compassion**

- Feeling overwhelmed by stress → Begin with **Mindfulness**

- Getting stuck in negative thinking → Focus on **Thought Reframing**

- Reacting before thinking → Practice **Emotional Awareness**

- Taking setbacks too personally → Develop a **Growth Mindset**

2. **When you face a difficult situation, you typically:**

- Blame yourself harshly → Self-Compassion will help most

- Feel physically stressed (racing heart, tension) → Mindfulness techniques will help

- Get caught in "what if" spirals → Thought Reframing is your priority

- React before understanding your feelings → Emotional Awareness is key

- Feel defeated or define yourself by the failure → Growth Mindset would serve you best

Start with the tool that addresses your most immediate need. Once that feels more natural, gradually incorporate the others. Remember, these tools work synergistically—the more you practice them together, the more resilient you become.

Picture yourself a few months from now, having practiced these skills regularly. Life hasn't become perfect -- there are still challenges at work or school, still occasional conflicts or setbacks (that's life!). But **you** are different in how you handle them. A challenge arises and you don't crumble; maybe your mind still tosses up an old negative thought or fear, but now you *notice* it and refuse to buy into it. You consciously reframe it and move forward. You encounter stress, but you remember to breathe deeply and regain your center. You face a disappointment, but instead of berating yourself, you treat yourself with compassion -- you rest, you encourage yourself to try again -- and you find you bounce back faster than before. You don't shy away from new opportunities or challenges out of fear of failure; instead, you might even seek them out, thinking, *"This will help me grow."* This kind of emotional resilience is like a superpower. It doesn't mean you'll never feel sad or angry or anxious -- of course you will, you're human. It means those feelings won't control you or stop you for long. You'll have the inner tools to navigate through them and come out the other side stronger.

Bridge to Chapter 5: From Inner to Outer Strength

As we conclude our exploration of mental mastery, we turn our attention to another vital aspect of well-being—the physical foundation that supports all your inner work. In Chapter 5, "Physical Well-Being and Energy: Strengthening Your Foundation," we'll discover how caring for your body enhances your ability to maintain emotional balance and mental clarity.

Just as you've learned to tend to your thoughts and feelings, your physical self deserves equal attention. Energy, sleep, nutrition, and movement all affect how you think and feel. When your body is strong and well-nourished, your mind works better too. You'll find it easier to implement the mental mastery practices you've just learned when your physical foundation is solid.

So let's continue our journey by exploring how to nurture the vehicle that carries you through life—your body. Together, a resilient mind and a vibrant body create the foundation for a truly fulfilled life.

5

— • —

PHYSICAL WELL-BEING AND ENERGY — STRENGTHENING YOUR FOUNDATION

The Wake-Up Call

Maya groaned as the alarm blared for the third time that morning. Her head throbbed, and her heart sank when she glanced at the clock. **7:45 AM.** "Oh no... not again," she whispered, leaping out of bed. Today was her son Aiden's school play—he had begged her to come watch him sing in the choir. It started at 8:30. Maya had planned to get up early, finish a work report, and then head to the school. Instead, here she was, running on five hours of fractured sleep, dehydrated from last night's caffeine, and scrambling to simply **be there** for her child.

She rushed through her morning routine—splashing cold water on her face, skipping breakfast (again), grabbing her keys. By the time Maya raced into the auditorium, the children were already taking their final bow to thunderous applause. She spotted Aiden on stage, his small face scanning the audience. *He doesn't see me*, she realized, chest tight with regret. In that crushing moment, Maya understood something had to change. It wasn't that she didn't love her son or her job—she loved them dearly. It was that **she had been neglecting the very foundation that allowed her to show up fully**: her own body.

Exhausted, undernourished, and perpetually running on fumes, she simply didn't have the energy or clarity to honor her intentions. Tears welled up as guilt and disappointment washed over her. How many times had her physical exhaustion led to broken promises? The missed morning workout that left her irritable all day, the brain fog that caused her to falter in a work meeting, the lack of energy to play with Aiden in the evening... it all added up.

That evening, after apologizing to Aiden with all her heart (and listening to his own excited recap of the play, which somehow hurt even more), Maya made a quiet vow. Sitting at her kitchen table, she closed her eyes and **imagined** the life she wanted: Being awake and present for precious moments. Bringing vibrancy and focus to her projects. Feeling *good* in her own skin. She realized that every part of that vision **depended on one thing** — a healthy, energized body.

In a flash of insight, she remembered something her late grandmother used to tell her: *"Take care of your body, and it will take care of you."* That night, Maya did something she hadn't done in years: she went to bed at 10 PM, leaving the dirty dishes in the sink and the TV off. It felt oddly empowering to choose rest over late-night distractions. It was the first small step in rebuilding her foundation.

"Your body is the vehicle through which you experience everything in life—treat it like the precious vessel it is."

Over the next weeks, Maya began treating her body with the respect it deserved. Mornings now started with a tall glass of water and a short walk in the sunlight. She established a gentle bedtime routine—dimming the lights and reading a few pages of an inspiring book before sleep. At first, the changes were challenging; her old habits tugged at her, urging her to watch just one more episode or check her email at midnight. But Maya remembered her promise. Little by little, she noticed her energy rising. She woke up before her alarm and watched the sunrise as she stretched her limbs, feeling **present and alive**. At work, she was more focused and patient. At home, she laughed more and snapped less.

One Saturday, Aiden declared, "Mom, you seem happier." Maya smiled, heart full, knowing *exactly* why. Her **physical well-being** was no longer an afterthought—it had become the bedrock of her daily life.

Like Maya, I've experienced my own wake-up call. Several years ago, while building my consulting business, I prided myself on "hustle culture" – sleeping just 4-5 hours to fit in more clients, skipping meals when busy, and reaching for caffeine and sugar to push through energy crashes. My wake-up call came during an important presentation to potential investors when my mind suddenly went blank mid-sentence. After an awkward pause and fumbled explanation, I barely made it through. The investors passed on the opportunity, and I knew something had to change. That humbling moment taught me that no amount of ambition can overcome a neglected body. Within three months of prioritizing sleep, nutrition, and movement, I closed a deal twice the size with much greater ease – all because my body and mind were finally working as a team.

TOOLKIT REFERENCE

To begin your own physical well-being transformation, see "Personal Energy Audit" and "Well-Being Baseline Assessment" in Section 5 of the Practical Toolkit.

Key Takeaway: Maya's story shows that caring for your physical well-being is not a selfish indulgence—it's an act of love that fuels **everything** else. No matter how big your dreams or how strong your motivation, if your body is running on empty, you'll be fighting uphill. But when you honor your physical foundation, you empower every other part of your self-development journey. As fitness legend Jack LaLanne said, *"Your body is your most priceless possession — take care of it."* And in the words of a wise saying, *"Discipline doesn't stop at your desk — it starts with how you sleep and move."* Strengthening your body is strengthening your *whole life*. With that in mind, let's explore the core pillars of physical well-being that will energize your transformation: **sleep, hydration, movement, nutrition,** and **body awareness**.

Physical Well-Being: The Amplifier of All Other Growth

Before diving into each pillar, let's understand why physical well-being is so crucial to your overall development. Your physical state doesn't exist in isolation—it directly impacts every other aspect of personal growth we've covered:

[PHYSICAL WELL-BEING CONNECTION DIAGRAM]

- **Self-Awareness (Ch. 1):** A rested, well-nourished brain has greater capacity for honest reflection and clarity of thought.

- **Values Alignment (Ch. 2):** Physical energy gives you the stamina to live according to your values instead of taking the path of least resistance.

- **Discipline (Ch. 3):** Your willpower is a biological function that depletes when your body is tired or undernourished.

- **Emotional Mastery (Ch. 4):** Physical state profoundly affects mood regulation—hunger, dehydration, and fatigue all amplify negative emotions.

This interconnection means that improving your physical well-being creates a positive upward spiral in all areas of your growth. Let's now explore each physical pillar in depth.

Prioritize Sleep: Recharge Your Body and Mind

Picture your body as a smartphone that needs recharging each night. Sleep is nature's **recharge button** — the time when your body repairs itself and your mind processes the day. Most adults need around **7-8 hours of sleep** each night for optimal health. Imagine trying to use your phone all day without ever charging it; that's what skimping on sleep does to your brain and body.

Far from being a luxury or laziness, **adequate sleep is a critical part of high performance**. In fact, getting enough rest helps reduce stress, stabilize your mood, and sharpen your thinking. Ever notice how problems seem bigger and emotions run higher when you're exhausted? On the flip side, after a good night's sleep you often wake up clearer, calmer, and more disciplined almost automatically.

One key to quality sleep is maintaining a **consistent bedtime and wake-up time**. Your body's internal clock (circadian rhythm) thrives on routine. Try to go to bed and get up at the same times each day (yes, even on weekends) so your body knows when to wind down and when to energize. Think of it as giving yourself the gift of a steady rhythm — much like the sun rises and sets on cue, your body loves predictability.

If you've been burning the midnight oil, start by gradually moving your bedtime up until you're hitting that 7-8 hour range. Create a simple **wind-down ritual** in the hour before bed: dim the lights, turn off screens, maybe do some light reading or journaling. Make your sleep environment comfortable — aim for darkness, quiet, and a cool temperature. **Protect this time as sacred**. Remember, discipline isn't just about working hard; it also means having the discipline to shut down and sleep when the day is done. (Think of our friend Maya, pushing away the laptop and choosing rest, as an act of discipline and self-respect.) It might help to remind yourself at night: *tomorrow's success begins tonight*. By prioritizing sleep, you're setting up tomorrow to be a win.

"Sleep isn't a luxury or an indulgence—it's the foundation upon which all your achievements are built."

Most importantly, **don't feel guilty** for giving your body the rest it needs. You are far more productive, emotionally balanced, and resilient when you're well-rested. As one health guide wisely puts it, getting 7+ hours regularly keeps your mind and body healthy. In a very real sense, sleep is an investment in your next day's success. So tonight, do yourself a favor — turn off the world, sink into your pillows, and let your body recharge. When you wake up refreshed, you're ready to **run the day instead of letting the day run you**.

Addressing Common Sleep Resistance

"But I don't have time for 8 hours of sleep!" This is perhaps the most common objection I hear. Consider this perspective shift: it's not about having time, but making time for what truly matters. Top performers like LeBron James and Jeff Bezos prioritize 8-10 hours of sleep despite their demanding schedules. Why? They recognize that sleep doesn't take away from productive time—it multiplies the quality of their waking hours. Would you rather have 16 mediocre hours or 14-15 high-quality, focused hours? Quality beats quantity every time.

"I've tried improving my sleep but still wake up tired." If you're sleeping adequate hours but not waking refreshed, consider factors like sleep quality and timing. Try eliminating screen use an hour before bed (the blue light disturbs melatonin production), maintaining a cooler bedroom temperature (65-68°F is optimal for most people), or consulting a doctor about potential sleep disorders like sleep apnea, which affects up to 20% of adults but often goes undiagnosed.

TOOLKIT REFERENCE

To transform your sleep quality, practice the "Sleep Environment Optimization" and "Evening Wind-Down Ritual" in Section 5 of the Practical Toolkit.

Practical Tips — Better Sleep Habits:

- **Set a Consistent Schedule:** Go to bed and wake up at the same times each day. Consistency trains your body to know when it's time to sleep and when it's time to be alert.

- **Create a Wind-Down Routine:** In the last hour of your day, ease into rest. Turn off electronics (the emails and shows can wait), dim the lights, and do something relaxing — read a book, take a warm shower, or practice deep breathing. This signals to your brain that it's time to slow down.

- **Optimize Your Sleep Environment:** Make your bedroom a sanctuary for sleep. Keep the room dark (consider blackout curtains or an eye mask), quiet (use earplugs or a white noise machine if needed), and cool (most people sleep best in a slightly cool room). Comfortable pillows and bedding can make a big difference too.

- **Guard Your Sleep Time:** Treat your sleep like an important meeting with yourself — because it is! That might mean politely saying no to late-night TV binges or social media scrolling. Remind yourself that you're not being weak for going to bed — you're being **wise**. You're fueling the mind and body that will conquer tomorrow.

Reflection Prompt: *Think about your current sleep routine. Are you giving yourself enough time to recharge? In your journal or mind, list one or two changes you could make to improve your sleep habits. Maybe it's setting an earlier bedtime, or establishing a no-screens-after-10 PM rule. How do you imagine better sleep will impact your mood and productivity the next day?*

Hydration: Fuel Every Cell

Each morning, after you open your eyes and stretch, your body is craving one essential ingredient: **water**. You've just gone 7-8 hours (hopefully!) without drinking anything, and every cell in your body is a bit parched. Hydration is the foundation that literally **fuels your cells** — it's like oil for the engine of your body.

Starting your day with a tall glass of water is one of the simplest yet most powerful habits you can adopt. In fact, neuroscientist Andrew Huberman emphasizes that even being **1% dehydrated** — a level so small you might not even feel thirsty — can significantly reduce your mental sharpness and physical performance. Think about that: a mere 1% deficit in water, and you're already slower, foggier, less vibrant than you could be. No wonder on days when you forget to drink enough, you end up with headaches or that infamous afternoon slump.

Hydration is truly foundational; if you consider your body an instrument, water is the tune-up that keeps all the strings in harmony.

One great morning tip (as we touched on in the "New Day" routine back in Chapter 3) is to add a **tiny pinch of natural salt** or a squeeze of lemon to your first glass of water. Why salt? Because it provides electrolytes that help your nerves and muscles function well, balancing the fluids in your body. Think of it as turbo-charging your hydration. This little hack can help your body actually *absorb* and utilize the water more effectively.

After that initial glass, make it a point to drink water consistently throughout the day. Don't wait until you're *really* thirsty — thirst is actually a late signal, a polite reminder that your cells needed water some time ago. A common guideline is to aim for about **8 glasses of water a day (roughly 2 liters),** but listen to your body and adjust based on your activity level and climate (on a hot day or after exercise, you'll need more). The key is regular intake: *little sips, all day long.*

During the day, consider carrying a water bottle as your trusty sidekick. It's a visual cue to sip often. Maybe set a reminder on your phone every couple of hours: "Hydrate!" — until it becomes an automatic habit.

"**Water is to your body what clean fuel is to a high-performance engine—the quality of what you put in determines how well you run.**"

Hydration isn't just about **quantity**; it's also about **quality**. Water-rich foods like fruits and vegetables contribute to hydration too (bonus: they come with vitamins and fiber). Herbal teas or diluted natural juices can count as well. On the flip side, be mindful with drinks that dehydrate — excessive coffee or sugary sodas can actually pull water out of you. It's not that you can't enjoy a cup of coffee (I certainly do), but balance is everything. Perhaps match each cup of coffee with an extra glass of water.

As you tune into your hydration, notice the changes: your skin might get a bit clearer, your focus a bit sharper, your mood a bit more even. Many people find that when they're well-hydrated, they don't hit that 3 PM energy crash as hard, and their overall sense of well-being improves. It's amazing how this basic act of self-care can have such profound ripple effects. **Water truly is life**. By hydrating, you're literally fueling every cell of your body with what it needs to operate at its best.

REAL-LIFE TRANSFORMATION: James, a software developer I coached, had suffered from chronic afternoon headaches for years. He drank 3-4 cups of coffee daily but rarely water. After one month of drinking 2 liters of water daily, his headaches disappeared completely. More surprisingly, his productivity skyrocketed—he was finishing code that previously took 8 hours in just 5-6 hours because his mind stayed sharp all day. "I spent hundreds on specialist appointments," he told me, "when the solution was basically free."

TOOLKIT REFERENCE

To establish effective hydration habits, use the "Hydration Tracking System" and "Flavor Infusion Guide" in Section 5 of the Practical Toolkit.

Practical Tips — Hydrate Like a Pro:

- **Morning Hydration Ritual:** Make it a habit to drink a large glass of water first thing in the morning, before coffee, breakfast, or checking your phone. This wakes up your system and compensates for the overnight fast. Add a pinch of sea salt or a squeeze of lemon to boost electrolyte balance and freshness.

- **Carry a Water Bottle:** Keep a reusable water bottle with you throughout the day — at your desk, in your bag, in the car. Having water always within reach makes you far more likely to sip regularly. If it's out of sight, it's out of mind; so keep it in sight!

- **Set Hydration Checkpoints:** Create little triggers for yourself: for example, decide that you'll drink a glass of water every time you finish a task, or at the top of each hour, or every time you take a break. These cues help integrate hydration into your routine.

- **Eat Your Water:** Remember that many foods are hydrating. Snack on fruits like watermelon, oranges, or grapes, and include vegetables like cucumber, lettuce, or soup in your meals. These not only hydrate you but also give you valuable nutrients.

- **Listen to Your Body's Thirst Signals:** Learn to recognize when your body is whispering for water. Early signs can be a slight dry mouth, a bit of fatigue, or a dip in concentration. Don't wait until you're parched; by then, your performance and mood may have already taken a hit. Keep ahead of the thirst.

Reflection Prompt: *On an average day, how much water do you think you drink? Consider tracking your water intake tomorrow. Note how you feel in the late afternoon: are you energized or dragging? Now imagine increasing your hydration — how do you think better hydration could affect your energy and clarity? Jot down one strategy you'll use to remind yourself to drink water regularly (e.g. setting a phone alarm or using a marked water bottle).*

Move Your Body: Exercise for Energy and Mood

Our bodies were designed to **move**. Yet, in modern life, it's easy to spend hours sitting — at a desk, in a car, on a couch. The result? Stiff joints, low energy, and often a stormier mood. Movement is not just about getting fit or reaching a certain weight; it's about **energy** and **emotion**. When you move your body, you change your state.

Tony Robbins often says, "Motion creates emotion," and it's true — ever notice how a brisk walk can lift your spirits, or a few stretches can release frustration? As Jim Rohn famously put it, *"Either you run the day, or the day runs you."* One powerful way to *run your day* is — quite literally — to **run (or walk, or dance, or stretch) at the start of it**. By starting your morning with movement, you send yourself a message: *I am in charge of my energy.*

You don't have to be a marathoner or a gym rat; the key is to find some form of movement that you **enjoy** and do it consistently.

Let's dispel a myth right now: when it comes to exercise, **consistency beats intensity** for beginners. It's far better to walk for 15 minutes every day than to do a 2-hour intense workout once a month. We're building a lifestyle, not punishing ourselves. So, commit to some form of movement **every single day** — think of it as daily maintenance for your body and mind.

This could be a 10-minute morning stretch while listening to music, a brisk walk around the block during lunch, or even dancing in your living room to three of your favorite songs. The trick is to make it enjoyable. When movement is a chore, it won't stick. When it's fun or deeply satisfying (like a peaceful bike ride in the park, or a playful game of tag with your kids, or a calming yoga session), it becomes something you look forward to.

And those minutes of movement pay off hugely. You'll notice it immediately: a short walk can shake off that grogginess or anxiety and replace it with clarity and calm. In fact, walking has been proven to relieve stress, lift your mood, and even improve sleep quality. One study found that a 20-minute walk can boost your energy *more* effectively than a cup of coffee — talk about an all-natural energy drink!

Those "feel-good" chemicals (endorphins) start flowing, and your whole outlook can shift. Instead of reaching for another espresso when the mid-afternoon slump hits, try a 10-minute stroll outside and see what happens. Your body will reward you with more sustained energy and a clearer mind.

Overcoming the "No Time" Barrier

"I hear you about exercise, but I honestly don't have time," is something I hear constantly. Here's the truth: you don't need to find time—you need to make time. And you need much less than you think. Studies show that even micro-workouts of 4-10 minutes can significantly improve health markers when done consistently.

Consider the "1% Rule": dedicating just 1% of your day to movement means 14-15 minutes out of 24 hours. Can you truly not afford that small investment for exponential returns in energy, mood, and long-term health? Try this perspective: movement isn't something that takes time away from your day—it gives time back through increased productivity, mental clarity, and years added to your life.

"Movement is like medicine—a daily dose keeps both your body and mind functioning at their best."

When you're just starting out, keep it simple. You might set a modest goal like **5,000 steps a day** (if you have a pedometer or smartphone app, great — if not, 5,000 steps is roughly a 30-40 minute walk). Or commit to **30 minutes of movement** in whatever form each day. Track it to keep yourself accountable — maybe jot it in your planner or use a habit-tracking app.

Treat it like a game: *Can I beat my step count from yesterday? Can I go one minute longer or a bit farther?* Celebrate each small win. If you walked for 10 minutes today, that's fantastic — it's 10 minutes more than nothing! Tomorrow, maybe you'll go for 12. Over time, these small acts compound. That 10-minute walk might turn into a 30-minute walk because you start to genuinely enjoy your quiet morning time. Or those gentle stretches might evolve into a desire to try a yoga class.

You'll find your **strength and endurance growing**, often to your own surprise. The human body is amazingly adaptive — give it movement, and it will respond by waking up muscles and systems you forgot you had.

TOOLKIT REFERENCE

To create a sustainable movement routine, use the "Enjoyable Movement Finder" and "Progress Tracking Template" in Section 5 of the Practical Toolkit.

Keep in mind, movement is as much for your **mind and soul** as it is for your body. Remember how in Chapter 4 we explored techniques for emotional mastery? Here's a secret: it's *easier* to master your emotions when your body has moved. If you're anxious or angry, a quick run, a series of jumping jacks, or even punching a pillow can safely release that tension and anger. If you're sad or sluggish, getting up and moving — even though it's the last thing you might *feel* like doing — can gently nudge you into a better mood.

I personally have a rule: when in doubt, **move** — even if it's just a walk around the block to clear my head. Nine times out of ten, I come back in a better mood or with a new insight. Use movement as an emotional reset button and a form of meditation. As you walk or jog, focus on the sensation of your feet on the ground, the air in your lungs. Let your mind wander and unwind. Some of the best ideas and solutions to problems will strike you **while your body is in motion** — it's no coincidence that great thinkers like Einstein were known to walk when they needed to solve a tough problem.

Practical Tips — Make Movement a Lifestyle:

- **Start Small and Build Up:** If you're not used to exercising, begin with *tiny* daily moves. Five minutes of stretching in the morning, a short walk after dinner — whatever feels doable. The important thing is doing it **every day**. Once it's a habit, you can gradually increase the time or intensity.

- **Find Activities You Love:** Hate running? Don't run. Maybe you love nature — try hiking on weekends. Enjoy music — dance in your living room. Like solitude — yoga or cycling might suit you. Love company — join a group fitness class or invite a friend to walk with you. There are endless ways to move; choose what brings you joy.

- **Sneak Movement into Your Day:** Not all exercise has to happen in one block. Take the stairs instead of the elevator. Park a bit further and walk. Do some squats or march in place while waiting for the microwave. These little bits add up, keeping your body active throughout the day.

- **Use Triggers and Cues:** Tie movement to existing habits. For example, do 5 minutes of stretching right after you brush your teeth in the morning. Or do a quick set of push-ups or a dance break every time you send an email. Make it almost automatic that way.

- **Listen to Your Body (and Heart):** Some days you might feel full of energy — great, maybe go for a longer walk or a bike ride. Other days you're sluggish — that's okay, do something gentle like stretching or just a slow stroll. The goal is consistency, not perfection. By moving in some way each day, you're telling your body *"I care."*

Reflection Prompt: *Recall a time you felt really good after being active — maybe a time you walked in the fresh air, or played a sport, or simply took a relaxing stretch. What was the activity and how did you feel afterward? Write down how you might recreate that feeling this week. What is one form of movement you enjoy (or think you could enjoy) that you can commit to doing tomorrow? Even if it's just for 10 minutes, schedule it in. How do you imagine you'll feel right after doing it, and later that day?*

Nutrition: Fuel Your Body, Don't Punish It

Nutrition can be a touchy topic for many of us. In a world of fad diets and conflicting advice, it's easy to develop an adversarial relationship with food—seeing it as the enemy, or as a guilty pleasure, or as something you "earn" through hard work. Let's wipe that slate clean right now. **Food is not your enemy, and it's not a morality test.** Food is **fuel** for your amazing body and brain. It's the nourishment that allows you to do everything you want to do — from thinking clearly, to lifting your kids, to pursuing your dreams.

When you shift your mindset from "What do I have to avoid or deny myself?" to "How can I fuel myself so I feel great and perform at my best?", you take a huge step toward a healthy, joyous relationship with eating.

Consider this simple truth: Your brain is *always* on, and it literally runs on the food you provide. Just like a high-end sports car needs quality gasoline, your mind and body thrive on high-quality foods. If you pour muddy, low-grade fuel into a Ferrari, it's going to sputter and stall. In the same way, if we routinely feed ourselves ultra-processed junk, excessive sugars, or greasy, nutrient-poor meals, our bodies and minds will eventually protest.

You might feel it as the classic "sugar crash," or the afternoon fatigue after a fast-food lunch, or even longer-term issues like sluggish thinking and low mood. In fact, research shows that diets high in refined sugars can impair brain function and worsen mood disorders. On the flip side, when you nourish yourself with whole, nutrient-dense foods — think colorful vegetables and fruits, lean proteins, whole grains, nuts and healthy oils — you're giving your body premium fuel.

Over time, you'll likely notice steadier energy, a brighter mood, and even a more positive outlook on life. It's hard to feel enthusiastic about your goals when you're bloated or riding a blood-sugar rollercoaster. But when your body is well-fueled, you wake up with more natural energy and drive.

"What you eat literally becomes you—choose foods that build the version of yourself you want to become."

Now, this isn't about being **perfect** or never touching a cookie again. Life includes pizza nights and birthday cakes, and that's okay! The goal is **balance and mindfulness**. Start by listening to your body's responses. Pay attention to how you feel after different meals. Maybe that heavy, creamy pasta leaves you lethargic and ready for a nap at 2 PM, whereas a lighter lunch with veggies, protein, and some complex carbs (like quinoa or brown rice) gives you steady energy through the afternoon. Or perhaps you notice you concentrate better on days when you've had a good protein-packed breakfast.

Everyone's optimal diet can vary a bit — some people feel great on mostly plants, others need a bit more protein or healthy fat — but a good general principle is: **eat foods as close to their natural state as possible**. An apple instead of apple juice. Grilled chicken instead of chicken nuggets. A handful of almonds instead of a candy bar. These small swaps mean more nutrients, more fiber, and fewer additives.

TOOLKIT REFERENCE

To develop a healthy relationship with nutrition, practice the "Food-Mood Tracking" and "Meal Planning Simplifier" in Section 5 of the Practical Toolkit.

It can also be really helpful to think in terms of **adding good stuff in**, rather than just cutting "bad" stuff out. The more you add nourishing foods, the more they *crowd out* the less healthy options. For example, challenge yourself to add an extra serving of vegetables to your dinner tonight. Or drink water instead of soda during one meal. Or swap chips for some carrots and hummus for your snack. These little upgrades, done consistently, become habits — and those habits shape your health. And guess what? When you're filling up on the good stuff, you'll find you naturally crave the junk less. Your taste buds can change over time; that candy bar might start tasting *too* sweet once you've gotten used to the natural sweetness of fruits.

The Game-Changing Habit: Food Prep

One of the most powerful strategies for consistent healthy eating isn't about willpower—it's about preparation. Consider this: when you're hungry, tired, or stressed, you'll almost always choose the easiest available option. If that's fast food or processed snacks, that's what you'll eat. But if you've prepped healthy options that are just as convenient, you'll choose those instead.

Try the "Sunday Prep" method: Spend 60-90 minutes one day a week preparing basics that make healthy eating easy all week. Wash and chop vegetables, cook a batch of lean protein, prepare hard-boiled eggs, portion nuts into grab-and-go containers. With these elements ready, throwing together a nourishing meal takes minutes—often faster than ordering delivery.

This strategy has helped countless clients transform their nutrition without feeling deprived. Remember: convenience usually trumps willpower. Set up your environment so the healthy choice is the easy choice.

Crucially, **drop the idea of punishing yourself with diet**. Eating a donut does **not** make you "bad," and eating a salad does not make you "good." There is no moral scoreboard. Nutrition is about nurturing, not judging. If you indulge in a treat, enjoy it fully and then move on — no guilt needed. What matters is what you do consistently. If 80% of the time you're making mindful, healthy choices that make you feel great, that 20% of treats or convenience foods won't derail you. In fact, allowing yourself flexibility can keep you from feeling deprived and falling into binge cycles.

Think of healthy eating as an act of self-respect and self-love. You're not eating the salad to punish yourself or because you "should" — you're doing it because you **care** about yourself and you want to *feel your best*. In Chapter 2, we talked about core values. If one of your core values is, say, vitality, growth, or self-respect, then fueling your body with proper nutrition is a direct expression of that value. Every time you choose a nutrient-packed meal, you're saying: *"I value myself, so I nourish myself accordingly."*

Let's get practical. One of the biggest obstacles to eating well is convenience. When we're busy or stressed, we'll grab whatever is easiest — which often is the packaged snack or fast food. So, plan ahead **to make the healthy choice the easy choice.** Perhaps on Sunday you spend an hour prepping some food for the week: grill some chicken or tofu, chop a bunch of veggies, cook a pot of brown rice or quinoa. Pre-portion some nuts or yogurt with berries for quick snacks. Stock your kitchen with wholesome options that are grab-and-go. Keep fruit visible on the counter. Store cut carrots, cucumbers, or celery sticks in the fridge at eye level, maybe with a tasty dip like hummus.

At work, stash some healthy snacks in your drawer (almonds, protein bars with natural ingredients, etc.). The idea is when hunger strikes, you have a good choice at your finger-tips and you're less tempted to reach for the bag of chips or the candy bar. Also, **don't skip meals** to "save calories" — that often backfires because you become so hungry later that it's hard to make a mindful choice. It's usually better to eat balanced meals at regular intervals so your blood sugar stays steady and you don't turn into that "hangry" version of yourself.

Practical Tips — Nourish Your Body:

- **Prioritize Whole Foods:** Base your meals around whole, unprocessed foods. Fill half your plate with vegetables and fruits of different colors (eat the rainbow!), include a source of protein (beans, fish, eggs, lean meat), and add some whole grains or starchy veggies for energy. Use healthy fats like olive oil, avocado, or nuts to add flavor and satiety.

- **Plan and Prep:** Take a little time each week to plan your meals and prepare ingredients. Even a simple plan like "Monday — stir-fry, Tuesday — pasta with veggies, Wednesday — chicken salad..." helps. Batch-cook things you can use for multiple meals (grains, roasted veggies, cooked protein). This way, healthy meals can be thrown together as easily as ordering takeout.

- **Smart Swaps:** Look for small swaps that make your favorite foods healthier. Love tacos? Use whole-grain tortillas and load up on fajita veggies. Crave something sweet? Try Greek yogurt with honey and berries instead of ice cream one night. Enjoy soda? Switch to sparkling water with a splash of fruit juice. Little changes add up.

- **Mindful Indulgence:** If you have a treat, truly savor it. Eat it slowly, enjoy every bite, and then let it go. No beating yourself up. Balance that treat with nutrient-dense foods in your next meals. Remember it's what you do most of the time that counts.

- **Listen to Your Body's Signals:** Pay attention to hunger and fullness cues. Eat when you're moderately hungry (not starving) and aim to stop when you're comfortably satisfied, not stuffed. Also notice how different foods make you feel. Your body often "votes" on your food choices with how it responds — more energy, sluggish, bloated, light, etc. Over time, you'll gravitate toward what makes you feel good.

REAL-LIFE TRANSFORMATION: Eliza, a marketing executive and mother of two, struggled with afternoon energy crashes that left her irritable with her family when she got home. "I was drinking three diet sodas a day and grabbing whatever was fastest for lunch—usually a bagel or fast food," she told me. After four weeks of making just two changes—replacing soda with water and bringing a prepared lunch with protein, vegetables, and healthy fats—her energy remained stable all day. "My team noticed I was sharper in late-day meetings, and my husband commented that I seem happier when I come home," she shared. "It wasn't about weight loss—it was about showing up as my best self for the people I care about."

Reflection Prompt: *Think about your eating habits over the last week. Can you identify one or two meals after which you felt **great** (energized, light, satisfied)? What were those meals? Now think of a meal that left you feeling sluggish or guilty. What was different? Jot down one positive change you could make to your diet this coming week — maybe add a veggie to your lunch, or replace a sugary snack with a piece of fruit. How do you think this change might improve your daily energy or mood?*

Body Awareness: Listen to Your Body's Wisdom

Your body is constantly sending you signals — little messages about what it needs or how it's feeling. But in our go-go-go culture, it's easy to tune them out. Developing the wisdom to **listen to your body** is a game-changer in self-care. Remember in Chapter 4, we discussed emotional awareness, learning to notice and name our feelings? Here we extend that awareness to the physical self.

It's often said that *"if you listen to your body when it whispers, you won't have to hear it scream."* In other words, pay attention to the subtle cues — the whispers — so that your body doesn't have to resort to shouting in the form of illness or burnout.

Start with basic signals: **hunger and thirst**. These might sound elementary, but how often have we all worked through lunch or ignored thirst because we were "too busy"? Don't wait until you're ravenous or parched to respond. Subtle cues like a dry mouth, a slight headache, or a dip in concentration might be your body's polite way of saying "I need water." Mood swings or irritability can be a blood-sugar alarm bell saying "I need food." (Ever heard the term *"hangry"*? It's real — hunger can morph into anger pretty quickly when we neglect it.)

By responding to these needs early — having a glass of water when you feel the first hint of thirst, eating a nourishing snack when your energy first dips — you prevent a bigger crash later on. It's like tending a fire: add a log *before* it burns down to embers, not after it's gone out.

"Your body speaks to you in whispers before it resorts to shouting—learn to listen to the whispers."

Next, pay attention to **fatigue and the need for rest**. We live in a society that often glorifies pushing through exhaustion. "Sleep when you're dead," the grind culture says. But that mindset is a recipe for breakdown. True strength includes knowing when to pause. If you've been exercising hard and you notice persistent muscle soreness or your performance is dipping, your body might be asking for a rest day or a lighter activity. If you've had an intense week at work and you feel mentally fried, give yourself permission to have an evening of doing nothing in particular — just relaxing, reading for pleasure, or going to bed extra early.

Rest is not laziness; **rest is part of growth**. Remember that muscles actually re-build and get stronger *during* rest periods, not during the workout. The workout is the stimulus; the rest is when the improvement happens. Similarly, our minds consolidate information and heal during downtime. If you never give yourself a break, you're actually limiting your growth. So listen when your body (or mind) whispers "I'm tired." That might mean taking a short nap, or it might mean taking a weekend off from any strenuous plans and just chilling.

TOOLKIT REFERENCE

To develop greater body awareness, practice the "Body Signals Inventory" and "Rest & Recovery Planning" in Section 5 of the Practical Toolkit.

Also, notice **tension and pain**. Our bodies often carry stress in physical ways — tight shoulders, clenched jaws, a knot in the stomach. These are signals too. For example, you might not consciously realize you're stressed about that upcoming presentation, but your neck and shoulders are up at your ears and your back is aching from the tension. Once you notice it, you can take steps: maybe do some shoulder rolls, take a few deep breaths, or go for a quick walk to ease the stress.

If you get a minor pain during exercise (say, a sharp twinge in your knee while jogging), don't just push through blindly. That doesn't mean you become paranoid about every little ache, but use common sense: pause, stretch, adjust your form, or rest if needed. Pain is often the body's way of protecting itself, asking you to pay attention. Treat these signals as you would feedback from a trusted friend. Instead of getting annoyed ("Ugh, why is my knee doing this to me!"), respond with care: *"Okay, my body's telling me something's off — let me address that."*

Over time, you'll develop a kind of intuitive dialogue with your body. You'll know that *good* muscle soreness means you had a productive workout, but a certain pinching pain is a red flag to get checked out. You'll recognize the difference between feeling lazy versus truly needing rest. This intuition is built by practice: the more you check in with your body, the better you understand its language.

Body Awareness Success Story

Let me share a powerful example of body awareness in action. Michael, a high-performing lawyer who worked with me, had experienced three anxiety attacks in six months. During our work together, he learned to do regular body scans throughout his day. "I discovered that hours before an anxiety spike, my body was already sending warning signals—tight chest, shallow breathing, clenched jaw—that I'd been completely ignoring," he explained.

Michael created a simple system: three times daily, he would pause for 30 seconds to scan his body. If he noticed tension, he'd take two minutes for deep breathing or a quick walk. These micro-adjustments prevented the tension from escalating. "I haven't had an anxiety attack in over a year," he reported. "I catch the warning signs early and make small corrections before things spiral."

His story illustrates how developing body awareness isn't just about comfort—it can be a crucial preventative health practice that improves both professional performance and quality of life.

Finally, appreciate the **two-way street between body and mind**. Our physical state affects our emotions, and our emotional state affects our body. We've all experienced this: when you're anxious, maybe your stomach churns or your heart races. When you're sad, your whole body might feel heavy. Conversely, when you're physically energized and strong, you tend to feel more confident and optimistic. And when you cultivate a calm mind through meditation or breathing, your muscles relax and blood pressure drops.

Knowing this, you can use your body to influence your mind. Feeling stressed? Maybe do a quick **body scan**: close your eyes and bring attention from head to toe, releasing any tension you find. Or try a few minutes of deep breathing — it signals your nervous system to calm down. Feeling down? Maybe do a few jumping jacks or step outside and stretch your arms to the sky — open posture can lift your mood a bit. The more you practice listening and responding, the more you'll find a harmonious balance. Your body becomes not a hurdle, but a partner in your personal growth.

"Your body's signals are its way of communicating wisdom—ignore them at your peril, listen to them for your prosperity."

Practical Tips — Tuning Into Your Body:

- **Morning Check-In:** When you wake up, take a moment before diving into your day. Ask yourself, "How do I feel this morning?" Scan your body from head to toe. Are you sore anywhere? Still tired? Feeling light and energized? Based on what you find, you might decide "I need a good stretch before breakfast" or "I pushed hard yesterday, so today will be a yoga and recovery day."

- **Scheduled Breaks to Breathe and Stretch:** Build tiny check-in moments into your day. For instance, every couple of hours at work, pause for two minutes. Close your eyes, roll your shoulders, unclench your jaw, and take a few deep breaths. Stand up if you've been sitting long. These micro-breaks not only release physical tension but also clear your mind.

- **Use Physical Signs as Emotional Clues:** If you notice physical stress signals like a headache or tight chest, consider what might be causing it emotionally. Are you anxious about something? Frustrated or overwhelmed? Once you identify it, address both levels: maybe journal about the worry (mind care) and do a gentle neck stretch or take a walk (body care).

- **Honoring Rest and Recovery:** Just as you plan your work or workouts, plan your rest. Maybe you set aside one evening a week as an "off" night — no strenuous activities, just relaxation. If you exercise regularly, ensure you have rest days or light days. Remember, downtime is not wasted time; it's where the healing and strengthening often happen.

- **Pain and Illness — Early Intervention:** If you feel a small ache or if you're coming down with something, respond early. Don't ignore that tickle in your throat — maybe up your vitamin C, rest more, hydrate extra. If your wrist hurts at the computer, adjust your posture or keyboard setup now, rather than after it becomes a chronic issue. Think of these responses as course-correcting before a minor issue becomes a major one.

Reflection Prompt: *Take a few minutes tonight to reflect on physical signals you've noticed recently. Have you felt frequent tension in a certain part of your body? What might that be related to in your life (stress at work, poor posture, unresolved worry)? Write down one "whisper" your body has given you lately. How can you respond kindly to it? Perhaps it's "I've been really tired every evening" — response could be "I'll aim to get an extra half hour of sleep." Or "My knees ache after long sitting" — response: "I'll take stretch breaks and strengthen the muscles around my knees." By acknowledging and acting on these whispers, you're building trust with your body.*

TOOLKIT REFERENCE

To deepen your body-mind connection, explore the "Body Whispers Journal" and "Physical-Emotional Connection Map" in Section 5 of the Practical Toolkit.

7-Day Challenge: Build Your Physical Foundation

Knowledge is powerful, but **experience** is where transformation truly happens. Now that we've covered the pillars of physical well-being — sleep, hydration, movement, nutrition, and listening to your body — let's put them into practice. I invite you to take on a **7-Day Challenge** to jump-start these healthy habits and experience the difference in real time.

- **Sleep 7-8 hours each night:** No ifs, ands, or buts — plan your evenings to make this happen. Choose a consistent bedtime that allows for a full night's rest and stick to it. Each morning, jot a quick note about how you feel after prioritizing sleep (you might be surprised at the boost in mood and clarity). Treat your bedtime like an important meeting with yourself that you **cannot miss**.

- **Walk/move for at least 30 minutes (or 5,000+ steps) daily:** The goal is consistent movement. You can break this up throughout the day. For example, a 10-minute walk in the morning, 10 minutes around lunch, and 10 in the evening works just as well as 30 minutes straight. Take the stairs when you can, stretch during TV commercials, play outside with your kids or pet — it all counts. The key is to get your body *in motion* every day. Record your activity each day (steps walked or minutes exercised) to see your progress. Celebrate each day you hit your target!

- **Drink at least 2 liters of water each day:** That's roughly eight 8-ounce glasses. Start with a big glass in the morning (yes, with that pinch of salt or squeeze of lemon if you like). Keep a bottle by your side and sip often. Perhaps set a goal like "finish one liter by lunch, second liter by dinner." Use any strategy that works — infuse water with fruit for flavor, use a marked jug, or tech reminders. Check off each day you reach your hydration goal.

"Seven days of consistent self-care can create more positive change than seven months of wishing for better health."

- **Fuel yourself with nourishing food:** For these 7 days, be mindful at each meal. Include at least one serving of vegetables or fruit **every day**. Aim to have balanced meals with some protein, healthy carbs, and fats. Also, identify one "junk food" or sugary drink habit that you're willing to cut back on this week — and swap it with a healthier alternative. (Maybe skip the afternoon soda and have herbal tea, or replace fries with a side salad at lunch.) The idea isn't to diet strictly, but to **consistently choose high-quality fuel** and minimize the stuff that makes you feel sluggish. Keep a simple food diary if that helps, or at least mentally note your wins (like "chose a home-cooked dinner over fast food — yay!").

- **Check in and reflect each day:** Each evening, take a minute to record how you're feeling — physically and mentally. This could be in a journal or a notes app, or even just a thoughtful pause. Did you have good energy throughout the day? How was your mood? How well did you focus? Any headaches or great moments of feeling strong? Also note any challenges: perhaps you had cravings or felt tired at some point — that's okay and normal. The point is to connect the dots between your habits and how you feel. For instance, you might realize, "On Day 3 I drank all my water and I didn't get my usual 3 PM headache!" or "After three nights of 8 hours sleep, I feel less anxious." These reflections will help cement your understanding of your body and motivate you to keep going.

TOOLKIT REFERENCE

To implement your 7-day challenge effectively, use the "Daily Well-Being Tracker" and "Physical Foundation Challenge Guide" in Section 5 of the Practical Toolkit.

It's just one week of your life — but you might be amazed at the changes you notice. Maybe by Day 4 you realize you're not needing that second cup of coffee because you're naturally more alert. Or your general mood is a bit calmer and happier. Perhaps you're sleeping more soundly by the end of the week. Pay attention to even the small positive shifts: fewer sugar cravings, less stiffness in the mornings, feeling a tad more upbeat, or even just the pride that comes from keeping a promise to yourself. **These are wins —** celebrate them!

After seven days, step back and review. Which habits made the biggest difference for you? What was hardest, and what came easier than expected? The real prize is if some of these habits stick beyond the week and start becoming part of your daily rhythm. Remember, the goal here isn't perfection; it's progress and awareness. You're learning how your body responds when you treat it well. And that experience is worth its weight in gold for your self-development journey. By undergoing this challenge, you're not just reading about change — you're living it.

Conclusion: Your Body — A Pillar for a Better Life

By completing this chapter, you've gained a deeper appreciation for your body as a **key pillar** in your personal growth journey. When you take care of it — when you sleep deeply, stay hydrated, move regularly, and eat mindfully — **everything else you've been working on gets a boost**. Your discipline strengthens (because you're practicing daily habits, and because a healthy body literally gives you more willpower and focus). Your emotional mastery improves (because you're not constantly battling fatigue or sugar crashes while trying to stay patient and positive). You find it easier to live in alignment with your values (because you're respecting the vessel that carries you through life, honoring that value of self-respect or vitality). In short, by caring for your physical foundation, you are amplifying every other area of your self-development.

Never forget the timeless wisdom shared by Jim Rohn: *"Take care of your body. It's the only place you have to live."* This body of yours is your lifelong home, the vehicle through which you experience **everything** — every hug, every sunset, every achievement, every challenge. It deserves your care and gratitude. You and your body are a team, and when you support that team with healthy choices, the payoff is a richer, more energetic life. Think of the difference: a day tackled by a well-rested, well-nourished, active you, versus a day slogged through by a tired, dehydrated, sugar-crashing you. It's almost a different person showing up! And that difference might be what turns a good life into a *great* life.

"Your physical well-being isn't just one aspect of your life—it's the foundation upon which all your dreams, relationships, and accomplishments are built."

As we close this chapter, take a moment to envision the **best version of yourself** — the you who has vibrant health and energy radiating from within. See that version of you pursuing your goals with enthusiasm, handling stress with grace, leaping out of bed in the morning ready to own the day. That vision is not far off. It's within reach, built one healthy choice at a time. You have already started laying those bricks in these past 7 days (and if you haven't done the challenge yet, you now have the blueprint!). Keep going. Make these physical well-being practices not just a one-week experiment, but a part of who you are. Someone who is energized, balanced, and **strong from the inside out**.

Remember Maya's story — her transformation began when she decided to honor her body. Yours can too. When you fuel your body with care, *life fuels you back*. You'll find you have more to give to your work, your loved ones, and your passions. Challenges won't feel as daunting when you're coming at them with a clear mind and a healthy body. Each good night's sleep, each glass of water, each walk in the sun, each nutritious meal — they are investments in **yourself**, compounding over time into a reservoir of strength and vitality.

Bridge to Chapter 6: From Individual Well-Being to Connection

As we move from caring for your physical foundation to the next chapter, "The Power of Connection," we'll expand our focus from internal well-being to the relationships that enrich our lives. Just as a healthy body supports all your endeavors, meaningful connections nourish your spirit and purpose.

In Chapter 6, we'll explore how your personal development journey isn't meant to be walked alone. The strength you've built—through honest reflection, clear values, disciplined habits, mental mastery, and physical vitality—now gives you a solid foundation from which to connect more authentically with others.

Think of it this way: you've been cultivating your inner garden, and now it's time to open the gate and share its fruits. When you're physically energized and mentally centered, you have more to give in your relationships. You can listen more attentively, give more generously, and establish healthier boundaries. Your connections become stronger because you're approaching them from a place of wholeness rather than neediness.

Let's discover how the work you've done on yourself can transform not just your inner experience, but also how you relate to everyone around you—from intimate partnerships to casual friendships, from family bonds to community involvement. The journey continues, moving from personal strength to the power of shared humanity.

6

— • —

THE POWER OF CONNECTION

*S*arah *leaned against the kitchen counter, phone in hand, staring at the screen with a heavy heart. It was 8 PM on the night of her big promotion. She should have been ecstatic—years of hard work had finally paid off. But as congratulations messages from colleagues lit up her phone, Sarah felt an unexpected emptiness. Who could she call to share the joy? In the past few years, she had canceled so many coffee dates and skipped so many family gatherings that she'd slowly drifted from her closest friends and loved ones. Standing there in the quiet of her apartment, she realized that her success felt hollow with no one to celebrate beside her. In that moment, Sarah made a promise to herself: she would reconnect and rebuild the relationships that truly mattered.*

The next day, she reached out to her college friend just to catch up—no agenda, no rushed "let's talk soon," but a real conversation. She called her dad and asked about his week, listening as he excitedly recounted a story she'd normally have been too busy to hear. She even joined a weekend hiking group to meet new people, pushing past her comfort zone to introduce herself and genuinely get to know others. At first, it felt awkward. Would her friends welcome her back? Did new people really want to connect? But each time Sarah made the effort, she was met with warmth. Over weeks and months, the group texts with friends started buzzing again; family dinners became a cherished Sunday ritual.

Sarah's life filled with laughter, support, and a sense of belonging she'd forgotten she needed. On her next work milestone, she didn't hesitate to invite a handful of friends to celebrate with her. The achievement meant so much more when she saw the pride and happiness on their faces, too. **Sarah's story is a powerful reminder:** accomplishments and challenges alike are richer when shared. Strong relationships aren't just a "nice to have"—they are the bedrock of a fulfilled life.

"The true measure of success isn't found in achievements you can list on a resume, but in the depth of relationships that make those achievements worth celebrating." — Original

TOOLKIT REFERENCE *To assess your current relationship landscape, see "Connection Inventory" and "Relationship Quality Assessment" in Section 6 of the Practical Toolkit.*

As it turns out, Sarah's realization is backed by research. A landmark Harvard study spanning eight decades arrived at a simple yet profound conclusion: *"Good relationships keep us happier and healthier. Period."* Not wealth, not fame—**relationships**. When we invest in our connections with others, we're not only adding joy to our days; we're literally supporting our mental and physical well-being. Now that you've strengthened your relationship with yourself in earlier chapters, it's time to bring that growth into your connections with others. Personal development was never a selfish pursuit—in fact, improving yourself **magnifies** your ability to connect with, lead, and support the people around you.

In this chapter, we'll explore how your inner work creates outer ripples, and how skills like empathy, communication, and setting boundaries can deepen your bonds. We'll look at how leading by example can elevate your relationships, the importance of surrounding yourself with uplifting people, and how to stay truly present in a hyper-connected (but often disconnected) digital world. Along the way, you'll find reflection prompts and exercises to turn insight into action. Let's dive in and discover how *connection* is the cornerstone of a happy, meaningful life.

THE RIPPLE EFFECT OF SELF-WORK ON OTHERS

Think of your personal growth like dropping a pebble in a pond—your inner work creates ripples that spread outward. When you've cultivated self-respect and self-love, you naturally show up with more empathy, patience, and understanding for others. You're less reactive and less needy, and more present and supportive. A healthy relationship with yourself radiates outward, elevating your friendships, family life, and even workplace interactions. Conversely, if you're constantly at war with yourself—filled with self-doubt or negativity—that inner turmoil can spill over and strain your relationships. In short, who you are to *yourself* sets the tone for how you are with *others*.

Let's be clear: personal development is **not** selfish. As motivational speaker Jim Rohn wisely put it, *"I'll take care of me for you, and you take care of you for me."* In other words, the best gift you can give those around you is to take responsibility for your own growth and well-being. When two people each stand on their own feet, they can walk forward together as stronger partners, friends, or teammates. Real connection isn't about clinging to someone to fill our voids; it's about two whole individuals supporting each other. Your inner strength becomes a stable foundation for every bond you build.

"Self-improvement is the most generous act—the better you become, the greater gift you are to everyone around you." — Original

Call to mind: have you noticed how your mood affects others? If you start the day smiling and optimistic, it often lifts those around you. If you're stressed or bitter, that energy can dampen the whole room. This is the ripple effect in action. By improving yourself, you're indirectly uplifting the atmosphere for everyone you meet. *We rise by lifting others*, and sometimes the first person we need to lift is ourselves. When your inner light is shining, you become a source of light for others. Your personal victories—overcoming a bad habit, achieving a goal, cultivating a positive mindset—inspire and encourage the people in your life, often in ways you may never fully know. Never doubt that the work you do on yourself has a positive effect on those around you, whether it's your children learning from your example or your friends catching your positive vibes.

TOOLKIT REFERENCE *To harness the positive ripple effect of your personal growth, practice the "Values Demonstration" and "Growth Impact Reflection" exercises in Section 6 of the Practical Toolkit.*

EMPATHY AND COMMUNICATION

Strong relationships are built on strong communication. As Jim Rohn said, *"If you just communicate, you can get by. But if you communicate **skillfully**, you can work miracles."* Communication is where your inner work meets the outer world—it's how you show your respect, empathy, and authenticity to others. Developing good communication skills can transform everyday interactions into meaningful connections. Let's highlight a few key elements of skillful communication that you can start practicing today.

Empathy & Understanding

Make a sincere effort to step into the other person's shoes. Imagine their perspective, feelings, and needs. Empathy is the heart of connection—it shows people that you truly care about what they're experiencing. This doesn't mean you must agree with everything someone says or does; it means you seek to *understand before being understood*.

For example, if a friend is venting about a tough day, empathy might mean resisting the urge to judge or immediately give advice, and instead simply acknowledging their feelings: "That sounds really difficult. I'm sorry you went through that." When you respond with empathy, you create a safe space for honesty. Empathy tells the other person *"I see you. I hear you. Your feelings matter."*

Active Listening

Listening is more than just hearing words—it's fully engaging with the speaker. That means putting away distractions, maintaining eye contact or nodding along, and really focusing on what they're saying instead of formulating your response. When you actively listen, your conversation partner feels heard and valued. In fact, research confirms that active listening helps people get on the same page and builds trust and empathy in relationships.

Try reflecting back what you heard to show you're truly tuned in ("So, what you're saying is..."). This not only ensures you understood correctly, but it also signals that you care. Remember the wise words often attributed to Maya Angelou: *"People will forget what you said, people will forget what you did, but people will never forget **how you made them feel**."* Making someone feel heard and understood is a gift they won't forget. Through empathy and active listening, you're essentially telling others, *"You matter to me, and I want to understand you."*

"Listening isn't waiting for your turn to speak—it's giving someone the rare gift of your full, undivided attention." — Original

Of course, communication isn't just about listening; it's also about how we express ourselves. Speaking truthfully and kindly, voicing our needs calmly, and even the tone we use all play a role. When you speak, strive for clarity and compassion. If something is bothering you, address it with respect rather than letting resentment build. If you appreciate someone, say it out loud. Good communication invites openness: when you communicate with empathy and honesty, you encourage the same from others.

TOOLKIT REFERENCE *To enhance your communication skills, practice the "Empathic Response Framework" and "Active Listening Checklist" in Section 6 of the Practical Toolkit.*

BOUNDARIES AND SAYING NO

Healthy communication isn't just about what you **say**—it's also about what you **don't allow**. This is where boundaries come in. Setting boundaries is how you teach others to treat you, and it's crucial for mutual respect. It's perfectly okay (and healthy) to articulate what you need or what is unacceptable to you in a relationship. Boundaries aren't walls to keep people out; they're guidelines that protect your well-being and foster respect.

For instance, if a friend consistently calls late at night and it disrupts your sleep, you might gently say, "I value our talks so much, but I need to get to bed by 10. Can we catch up earlier instead?" A true friend or caring family member will understand and respect that limit. By communicating your boundaries, you prevent frustration and resentment from simmering beneath the surface.

Along with boundaries comes the courage to say **"no"** when you need to. Many of us are habitually inclined to people-please—we say yes to invitations, favors, or extra responsibilities because we fear disappointing others. But constantly saying yes while neglecting your own needs often leads to burnout and quiet resentment. Remember: every time you say yes to something you don't truly want or have capacity for, you are inadvertently saying no to something else (often your own peace or priorities).

It's not unkind to decline a request when necessary—it's an act of honesty and self-respect. In fact, learning to say no can dramatically improve your mental health and relationships. As one therapist noted, protecting your time and energy by saying no *"encourages healthier and more balanced relationships."* When you set these limits, you're being authentic about what you can give. And when you do choose to say yes, you'll be able to give it your whole heart, without bitterness, because you're not stretched too thin.

"A 'no' spoken from self-respect is more valuable than a 'yes' given from fear or obligation." — Original

If "no" feels scary at first, start small. You can be polite yet firm: "I'm sorry, I can't make it this time," or "I have too much on my plate to take that on." You don't always owe a lengthy explanation. Remember that you're saying no to the request, **not** rejecting the person. Most importantly, remind yourself that it's not selfish to prioritize your well-being—when you take care of you, you can show up better for others.

As you practice setting boundaries and saying no, you'll likely notice an empowering shift: your relationships become more balanced, and you feel more in control of your time and energy. The people who truly care about you will respect the boundaries you set; those who consistently don't may be showing you that the relationship itself needs re-evaluation.

When you put it all together—listening fully, speaking with empathy, and asserting your needs kindly—you'll find that communication becomes like oil in the engine of a relationship, reducing friction and helping everything run smoothly. Over time, these skills become habits that transform the quality of your interactions. Next time you're in conversation, practice these tools: listen more than you speak, respond with understanding, and be clear about your needs or limits. You'll be amazed at how much more connected and respected you feel, and how you set the tone for healthier communication all around.

TOOLKIT REFERENCE *To establish healthy boundaries, use the "Boundary Definition Exercise" and "Graceful No Practice" techniques in Section 6 of the Practical Toolkit.*

LEADING BY EXAMPLE IN RELATIONSHIPS

You don't need a title to be a leader in your relationships. **Relational leadership** means guiding and uplifting others through your actions and example. The people around us, especially those closest to us, often take cues from how we behave. When you've been working on yourself—practicing honesty, kindness, and discipline—others can't help but notice. By "showing up" as your best self consistently, you inspire others to rise as well. In this way, your personal growth becomes a quiet form of leadership that can elevate everyone in your circle.

Think about a family setting or a team at work: one person who stays calm under pressure can influence everyone else to stay level-headed. If you handle conflicts with patience and respect, it encourages those around you to communicate in kind. If you admit your mistakes and take responsibility for them, it makes it easier for others to do the same. This is leading by example in everyday life—modeling the behaviors and attitudes you hope to see in others.

Actions speak louder than words, especially in relationships. You can talk about values or give advice all day, but ultimately people pay more attention to what you **do**. (Psychologists often note that children learn not by what parents *say*, but by what parents *model*. The same holds true for how all people learn from each other.)

"The most powerful way to change the relationships around you isn't through demands or lectures, but through living as the person you wish others would be." — Original

If you want a culture of honesty in your friend group, be truthful and keep your promises. If you want more positivity around you, avoid gossip or constant complaining. Be the first to do the thing you wish others would do—whether it's apologizing when you're wrong, expressing appreciation, or staying optimistic in tough times. Your example is contagious. Albert Schweitzer put it well: *"Example is not the main thing in influencing others. It is the only thing."*

By living out the qualities you value, you become a lighthouse for others: your integrity, compassion, and resilience shine a light, showing people what's possible. This isn't about being perfect or "better" than anyone—it's about authentically embodying the qualities you wish to see in your relationships. Over time, you'll find you've attracted like-minded people and even helped elevate those already around you.

Reflect for a moment: Have you ever had a friend whose dedication (to fitness, learning, or any passion) rubbed off on you, motivating you to step up your own game? Or perhaps you decided to break a bad habit, and then a family member, seeing your progress, felt inspired to try as well. When you lead yourself well, you lead others by default. By becoming the best version of you, you give others permission and inspiration to do the same. This is the ripple effect of self-work we discussed, in full force. **Lead by example**, and watch how it encourages growth in your friends, family, and colleagues. It's one of the most profound ways you can positively influence the world around you—one person at a time, starting with yourself.

TOOLKIT REFERENCE *To strengthen your relational leadership, practice the "Values Demonstration Plan" and "Positive Modeling Exercise" in Section 6 of the Practical Toolkit.*

BUILDING UPLIFTING CONNECTIONS

Just as you aim to be a positive influence on others, it's equally important to surround yourself with people who lift **you** up. Jim Rohn famously said, *"You are the average of the five people you spend the most time with."* Think about that for a moment. Who are the five people you interact with most frequently? How do they affect you? Do they inspire you, support your growth, and encourage your best qualities? Or do they drain your energy, enable your bad habits, or keep you stuck in negative thinking?

Sometimes, personal growth involves making tough choices about the company you keep. This doesn't mean abruptly cutting off long-time friends or judging others harshly; it means being mindful and **intentional** about your inner circle. Prioritize relationships that are mutually nourishing—people who celebrate your successes, empathize with your struggles, and lovingly challenge you to be your best. Seek out friends who share your values of growth and positivity.

This might even mean finding mentors or peers who are a few steps ahead of you in an area you're working on. A mentor could be an older friend, a teacher, a colleague, or anyone you admire with more life experience. Learning from them can accelerate your development and show you new possibilities. Likewise, growth-minded friends—those who are also dedicated to improving themselves—can be incredible allies. You motivate and hold each other accountable, creating a positive feedback loop of encouragement.

"Choose your inner circle carefully—these are the people who will either fan the flames of your potential or slowly extinguish them." — Original

On the flip side, if you recognize that certain relationships in your life are consistently toxic or one-sided, it may be time to set firmer boundaries or spend a bit less time with those individuals. For example, maybe you have an acquaintance who only calls to complain and never listens, or someone who belittles your dreams or values. Interactions like that can weigh you down. It's okay to create distance from people who repeatedly hurt or drain you. Protect your mental and emotional space—remember, you have the right to choose who gets the most access to your energy.

This might mean spending less time with the friend who leaves you feeling exhausted or politely disengaging from gossip sessions at work. Instead, invest more time in relationships that uplift you. Maybe schedule regular coffee dates with the friend who always leaves you energized, or join a community (in-person or online) that shares your positive interests and goals.

And don't overlook the power of **gratitude** in your existing relationships. Often we have wonderful, supportive people in our lives whom we unintentionally take for granted. Make it a habit to express appreciation. Tell your spouse or partner what you love about them, or thank a friend for always being there. A simple "I'm grateful to have you in my life" can strengthen a bond immeasurably.

Research shows that expressing gratitude can help initiate, maintain, and strengthen relationships—making them closer and more satisfying. In fact, regularly expressing gratitude has been linked to higher relationship satisfaction and a greater sense of connection between people. So whether it's a quick text saying, "Thinking of you, thank you for being such a great friend," or a heartfelt conversation, let people know the positive impact they have on you. It makes them feel valued, and it often encourages them to reciprocate the kindness, creating an upward spiral of mutual appreciation.

In building uplifting connections, **quality matters more than quantity**. A few truly supportive, positive relationships are worth more than dozens of superficial ones. Cherish the people who bring out your light, and strive to be that person for them as well. Celebrate their wins, stand by them in tough times, and keep inspiring each other to grow. When your social circle is filled with mutual respect, trust, and inspiration, every challenge feels more surmountable and every joy feels more profound.

TOOLKIT REFERENCE *To cultivate uplifting relationships, use the "Relationship Energy Audit" and "Gratitude Expression Practice" in Section 6 of the Practical Toolkit.*

NAVIGATING THE DIGITAL WORLD WITH PRESENCE

In today's world, one of the biggest barriers to deep social connection can be the little device in your pocket. Our smartphones and constant social media feeds often pull us away from the present moment with the people physically in front of us. Have you ever been talking to someone who keeps glancing at their phone? It doesn't feel great—it's as if you're competing for attention with a screen. We've all been guilty of this to some extent. The good news is that becoming aware of this habit is the first step to changing it.

Setting digital boundaries is about making conscious choices so that technology enhances rather than hinders your relationships. For instance, when having dinner or engaging in a meaningful conversation, consider putting your phone on silent and out of sight. Psychologists have found that even the mere presence of a phone on the table can reduce the quality of connection—people report feeling less close and less trustful when a phone is visible, even if it's not in use. The message (even if unintended) is "you're not my sole focus right now." By removing that phone from sight, you're silently saying, *"I'm here with you. You have my full attention."*

"True connection happens in the absence of screens—when eyes meet, voices are heard, and presence is felt without digital interruption." — Original

Try creating small tech-free rituals. Maybe you and your family decide to have an hour in the evening with no phones, or you agree that when you meet a friend for coffee, you'll both keep your phones tucked away. If someone does need to be on their device (say, an urgent call or a quick check of something important), acknowledge it and pause the conversation until you can both be present again. Being fully present is one of the greatest gifts you can give in any relationship. It tells the other person, *"You matter. This moment with you matters."*

Also, be mindful of social media usage, especially when you're in the company of others. Scrolling aimlessly in front of your partner or friends can rob you of real-life moments. Yes, checking updates is tempting (those apps are designed to grab our attention!), but ask yourself: *Is what's on my screen more important than the human being next to me?* Usually, the answer is no. By setting a boundary like "no social media when I'm hanging out with loved ones," you'll find your interactions become richer and more satisfying.

Another aspect of digital presence is knowing when to disconnect in order to truly connect. If you're spending quality time with loved ones, consider logging out of work email or silencing work-related notifications so your mind isn't pulled away. If you're accustomed to constant connectivity, this might feel odd at first, but you'll likely notice you feel more relaxed and engaged in the moment.

Remember, the goal isn't to demonize technology—it's to use it intentionally. A phone call or video chat can *deepen* a relationship if used to bridge distance or maintain contact with someone far away. Just don't let virtual connections **replace** or constantly **interrupt** the real connections right in front of you. It's all about balance. Use technology as a tool to connect (like setting up that reunion via group text or sharing photos with family abroad), but not as a crutch that prevents you from being present. By practicing digital mindfulness, you're saying to your friends and family: *"I value our time together more than any notification."* In a hyper-connected era, the ability to be fully present has become a superpower for building strong, trusting relationships.

TOOLKIT REFERENCE *To manage technology in your relationships, practice the "Digital Boundary Setting" and "Presence Practice" exercises in Section 6 of the Practical Toolkit.*

REFLECTION PROMPTS AND EXERCISES: STRENGTHEN YOUR CONNECTIONS

Knowledge is wonderful, but action is what truly transforms our lives. Now it's time to put these ideas into practice. Here are three practical exercises to help solidify your learning and enhance your relationships and social skills. **I encourage you to actually try these**—they might feel a little uncomfortable at first, but they're powerful steps toward real growth.

1. Reflect & Journal on a Key Relationship

Identify one relationship in your life that you feel could be stronger or where there's some tension. It could be with a family member, a friend, or a colleague. Set aside 15 minutes to journal about it. Ask yourself: *What do I appreciate about this person? What challenges or negative patterns exist between us?* Be honest and compassionate in your reflection.

Now, think about the communication tools from this chapter. Write down one specific change you will make in how you interact with them. Maybe you'll practice deeper listening during your next conversation, or perhaps you need to set a gentle boundary (for example, expressing your needs calmly or saying no to something that's been weighing on you). Describe how you plan to apply this new approach.

Action: In the coming week, put this into practice during an interaction with that person. Afterwards, jot down any differences you noticed in how you felt or how the other person responded. What did you learn from the experience?

2. Express Gratitude to Someone in Your Life

Choose one person you deeply value—someone who has supported you, inspired you, or simply been a positive presence. It could even be someone you haven't thanked in a long time (or ever!). Your task is to express your gratitude to them in a sincere and concrete way. This could be a handwritten letter, a thoughtful email or text, or a voice message—whatever format feels right to you.

The key is to be specific: tell them *what* you appreciate about them or recall a moment when their actions meant a lot to you. For example, you might write, *"Mom, I realize I never properly thanked you for always believing in me during college. Your confidence in me gave me strength when I doubted myself. I am so grateful for that."* Deliver the message to them—and if you can, do it in person or over a call so it's more personal.

Action: After expressing your gratitude, notice how this act makes you feel and how the other person reacts. Did this deepen your connection in some way? Often, expressing thanks boosts our own happiness and strengthens the bond on both sides.

3. One-Day Social Media Detox (Presence Challenge)

Plan a 24-hour period sometime soon (perhaps this weekend or a day you're off work) to do a mini "digital detox." For one whole day, avoid social media and any unnecessary phone use. If possible, extend this to avoiding any screen time except what's absolutely needed (like essential calls or if you must use GPS for directions). Use that day to **fully engage** with the people around you or to reconnect in other ways.

Maybe you schedule a meetup with a friend, play with your kids or pets, take a long walk with your partner, or even strike up a friendly conversation with a neighbor you usually only wave to. If you live alone or can't physically meet someone that day, use the time to call or video chat with someone you care about—give them your undivided attention. The goal is to notice how present you can be without the constant pull of online activity.

Action: At the end of the day, journal for a few minutes about the experience. How did you feel throughout the detox? What did you do to fill the time you'd normally spend scrolling or checking your phone? How did your interactions (with others or even just with yourself) feel compared to a normal day? What was hard about this, and what was surprisingly refreshing? This exercise can be eye-opening. You might even decide to make "tech-free days" a regular habit (say, a "Screen-Free Sunday") to regularly realign with what truly matters.

"Small acts of authentic connection can transform relationships more power-fully than grand gestures ever could." — Original

CONCLUSION & CALL TO ACTION

Remember, your personal growth amplifies your interpersonal growth. By working on yourself, you've lit a lamp inside—now let it shine outward. Strong relationships and social skills are really extensions of the respect, empathy, and confidence you've been cultivating within. Great relationships don't just "happen"; they're created through intention, care, and practice. The payoff? A richer, happier life for you and for everyone you care about. As the Harvard study showed, nurturing positive relationships isn't just a feel-good suggestion—it's a cornerstone of long-term happiness and health.

So here's my challenge to you: **Take action.** Don't just read these ideas—live them. Try the exercises above. Practice the new communication techniques you've learned. Reach out to someone today and invest a little extra energy into that connection. Lead with your example and positivity. Set a healthy boundary where you need one. Put the phone aside and truly listen. These small choices, made consistently, will transform the landscape of your relationships over time.

You've strengthened your relationship with yourself in earlier chapters—now is the time to let that strength flow into every connection you have. Be the friend, partner, family member, or teammate you aspire to be, one small step at a time. Remember that your growth is not just your own—it's a rising tide that lifts everyone around you. As you grow, you give others permission to grow as well.

BRIDGE TO CHAPTER 7: FROM CONNECTION TO PURPOSE

As we conclude our exploration of meaningful relationships, we turn our attention to a question that naturally emerges when we're connected to ourselves and others: What is it all for? In Chapter 7, "Purpose and Direction: Designing Your Life," we'll discover how to channel your self-awareness, values, discipline, emotional mastery, physical well-being, and relational skills toward a life of meaning and intention.

Having built connections with others, you're now ready to connect with something larger than yourself—a purpose that gives direction to your days. You'll learn to design a life that reflects your deepest values and aspirations, one where your actions align with a vision that truly inspires you.

Think of it this way: if the previous chapters were about building your foundation and creating your support system, the next chapter is about charting your course forward. With your internal compass calibrated and your relationships strengthening you, you're perfectly positioned to define where you want to go and why—to create a life by design rather than by default.

Let's discover how to transform all your personal growth work into a meaningful direction that makes your journey not just fulfilling in the moment, but purposeful for a lifetime.

7
— · —

PURPOSE AND DIRECTION — DESIGNING YOUR LIFE

"Now What?" — Finding Purpose After Personal Growth

Marcus stood on his porch that humid August evening, the weight of accomplishment strangely hollow in his chest. The past months had transformed him—he'd established healthy habits, cut toxic routines from his life, even rekindled old friendships that had withered under neglect. By any measure, he had become a better version of himself.

Yet as the cicadas hummed their evening song and dusk painted the sky in deepening shades of purple, a question kept surfacing in his mind: *Now what?*

The realization struck him with crystal clarity. He had climbed many rungs of life's ladder only to discover it might be leaning against the wrong wall. His grandfather's wisdom echoed in his memory—how the old man had reached the pinnacle of his career only to find emptiness where fulfillment should have been.

As Stephen Covey warned, **"If the ladder is not leaning against the right wall, every step we take just gets us to the wrong place faster."**

In that quiet moment of reflection, Marcus felt the nagging emptiness of a journey without destination. Despite all his hard-won improvements, they might lead nowhere meaningful without a purpose, a vision to guide them.

The next morning, Marcus woke with new resolve burning in his heart—to take control of his life's direction rather than drift aimlessly through his days. He remembered words from his mentor Jim Rohn that suddenly felt profound in their simplicity: **"If you don't design your own life plan, chances are you'll fall into someone else's plan. And guess what they may have planned for you? Not much."**

With those words ringing in his mind, Marcus decided right then to become the architect of his future. Fresh journal in hand, he began sketching what he **truly** wanted from life—not what others expected, but what **he** deeply yearned for. That simple act of defining direction felt like a weight lifting from his shoulders, replacing anxiety with electric anticipation.

Just as night gives way to dawn, Marcus's story illustrates a powerful truth: after laying the groundwork of personal growth, the next crucial step is aiming it all toward a **purposeful destination**.

"**Without purpose, even the most disciplined person is just efficiently going nowhere in particular.**"

TOOLKIT REFERENCE *To begin clarifying your life's purpose, see "Personal Purpose Discovery" and "Vision Quest Exercise" in Section 7 of the Practical Toolkit.*

The Importance of Long-Term Vision and Purpose

We all reach moments like Marcus's porch step epiphany. You might improve yourself in countless ways, yet still feel adrift until you define *why* you're doing it all. Having a long-term vision—a clear purpose—is like having a North Star on a dark night. Without it, even your best efforts can lead in circles.

History and wisdom tell us that purpose is no luxury; it's essential. President John F. Kennedy put it plainly: "**Efforts and courage are not enough without purpose and direction.**" No matter how fast you run, if you're on the wrong road you won't reach the destination that fulfills you. A person without purpose is often compared to a ship without a rudder, at the mercy of winds and currents. When we lack direction, life's inevitable storms can capsize us; with a guiding purpose, we can steer through rough seas.

Consider your own life: have you ever achieved a goal—a promotion, a degree, a fitness milestone—and then found yourself asking, "Is this it?" A long-term vision prevents that emptiness by ensuring your ladder is firmly set against the **right wall** from the start. It infuses your actions with meaning. As you clarify your purpose, you give yourself a reason to persevere through challenges that arise. Friedrich Nietzsche famously observed, "**He who has a why to live can bear almost any how.**" When your *why* is strong, setbacks don't defeat you—they refine you.

This chapter is about defining that motivating *why* for yourself: identifying a compelling vision for your life so that all your day-to-day efforts add up to something truly meaningful. Remember, "**The purpose of life is a life of purpose.**" In the pages ahead, we'll transform your values and dreams into a concrete life design. It's time to answer *"Now what?"* with confidence and chart your path forward.

"A purpose isn't something you find once and forever—it's something you refine and recommit to daily through the choices you make."

The Sara Blakely Story: Purposeful Vision in Action

Before we dive into creating your own vision, let's look at how purpose and direction transformed the life of Sara Blakely, founder of Spanx. Her story perfectly illustrates how a clear vision, aligned with values and pursued with determination, can lead to extraordinary outcomes.

In 2000, Sara was selling fax machines door-to-door. Frustrated with uncomfortable pantyhose in Florida's heat, she cut the feet off a pair to wear under white pants for a smoother look. This simple solution sparked an idea that would revolutionize the shapewear industry.

What's remarkable isn't just her invention, but how her clear purpose guided her through countless obstacles. Despite having no business, fashion, or retail experience, Sara was driven by a vision larger than just selling undergarments. Her purpose was to help women feel confident and comfortable in their clothes. This "why" sustained her through more than two years of rejection, setbacks, and challenges.

When manufacturers refused to take her seriously, when retailers were hesitant to stock her product, when she had to use her $5,000 life savings to start the company, her unwavering vision kept her moving forward. She wasn't just selling a product; she was pursuing a purpose that resonated deeply with her own values of empowerment and innovation.

The results speak for themselves: Spanx became a billion-dollar company, and Sara became one of America's youngest self-made female billionaires. But more important than the financial success is what her story teaches us: a clear purpose creates resilience. It transforms obstacles from roadblocks into stepping stones.

Sara once shared: "I always think about 'What is my why? Why am I doing this?' I did not go into this to make money... I went into this to solve a problem." This clarity of purpose guided every decision, from product development to company culture.

As you develop your own vision and purpose, remember Sara's example. Your "why" becomes your compass when the path gets rocky, your fuel when motivation runs low, and ultimately, the defining force that shapes your journey's destination.

Designing Your Ideal Future Life (Your Vision)

Imagine it's a few years from today—say 1, 3, or 5 years ahead—and you wake up living your ideal life. What's different? Where are you, who are you with, and what does your day look like? This imagined future is your **personal vision**, and it will serve as your guiding star. Without a clear vision, it's all too easy to wander aimlessly or climb someone else's ladder. As the Stoic philosopher Seneca wisely said, *"There is no favorable wind for the sailor who doesn't know where to go."* In other words, if you don't have a destination in mind, no amount of effort or "wind" will get you where you want to be.

Designing your ideal future life is about choosing a destination that truly **excites and fulfills you**—one aligned with your deepest values and aspirations.

Start by taking a panoramic look at your life. Envision the future *in each major area*: **Career, Relationships, Health, Personal Growth, Community,** and **Finance**, or any domains that matter to you. Dare to dream big and **be specific**. Perhaps in your career vision you see yourself running a creative business that you're passionate about. In your relationships, maybe you imagine a warm, balanced family life or a wide community of supportive friends. How about personal growth—do you see yourself speaking a new language, or having a degree, or mastering a skill you've long wanted to learn?

Don't just list outcomes—**picture the actual life**. What kind of home environment do you wake up in? What's the first thing you do each morning? Who do you spend your evenings with? The more vivid and concrete your vision, the more powerfully it will motivate you. This isn't about crafting a fantasy to escape into; it's about articulating a **North Star** that pulls you forward.

TOOLKIT REFERENCE *To create a detailed vision of your ideal future, practice the "Future Day Visualization" and "Life Domain Mapping" exercises in Section 7 of the Practical Toolkit.*

Now ground that vision in your **core values**. Think back to the values you hold dearest (perhaps you identified these earlier in your journey). Our values are the essence of what matters to us—like honesty, freedom, family, creativity, service, health, and so on. A compelling life vision is one that *reflects your values in action*. For example, if one of your top values is *freedom*, and you currently feel constrained by a 9-to-5 job, your ideal future might involve working remotely on your own schedule or being your own boss. If you deeply value *community*, your vision might include being an active leader or volunteer in a local group.

When your long-term vision resonates with your values, it generates an inner fire that keeps you going. You're not chasing someone else's idea of success, but **your own definition of a fulfilling life**. As you visualize your future, check that each element connects to something you truly care about. This is how we ensure our vision isn't just *impressive*, but deeply *meaningful*.

Take some time to actually **write down** a description of your ideal life. This will become your personal vision statement. Write it in the **present tense**, as if you are already living that life—this helps trick your mind into believing and embracing it. You might begin with a phrase like, "It is April 2030, and I am waking up to..." Describe your day and surroundings: What does a fulfilling day in that life include? Who is with you? What work or creative activities fill your time? How do you feel as you go about it?

Don't worry about making it perfect prose; focus on capturing what **matters most** to you. For example, a vision might sound like: *"It's five years from now, and I run my own design studio from a home overlooking the ocean. I start my day doing yoga on the balcony (health and peace of mind), then dive into creating projects for clients I'm passionate about (creativity). I have the flexibility to pick up my kids from school and spend quality evening time with family (family and love). I'm also mentoring two junior designers online (growth and contribution). Each day feels purposeful and energizing."* This sample paints a clear picture and, importantly, ties back to values in parentheses. Your vision should be **authentic to you**—there are no right or wrong answers, only what inspires you deeply.

"The clearer your vision of tomorrow, the more meaningful your actions become today."

Reflective Exercise — Craft Your Vision: Grab a journal and create a space for your imagination to roam. Use these prompts to shape your vision:

- **Project Yourself Forward:** Choose a future timeframe (for example, 3 years from today). Imagine a specific date in that year. Write, "It is [Future Date], and I am..." then let the story flow.

- **Describe Your Day:** In present tense, narrate a day in your ideal life. Where are you waking up? What does your morning routine involve? What meaningful work or activities do you engage in during the day? How do you spend the evening, and with whom?

- **Highlight What Matters:** Ensure the key elements of this life tie back to your core values. (If *growth* is a value, perhaps you mention ongoing learning or a creative pursuit. If *security* is a value, maybe financial stability features in your vision.)

- **Feel the Emotions:** Write about how living this life makes you feel. Do you feel joyful, challenged, peaceful, inspired? Our emotional reactions can reveal whether the vision truly resonates. Also ask *"Why does this life matter to me?"*—perhaps it allows you to make an impact or leave a legacy that's important to you.

Take 10-15 minutes for this exercise—write freely without self-editing. When you're done, read over your vision statement. Does it excite you? **It should**. A great vision gives you butterflies in your stomach and a fire in your heart. If it's not quite there, that's okay—you can refine it over time. The goal is that when you read it, you feel a surge of motivation and clarity about where you're headed. Keep this vision statement somewhere accessible—it's going to be the cornerstone for the goals and plans we create next.

Setting Meaningful Long-Term and Short-Term Goals

With a vivid personal vision in hand, you've answered the "where to go" question for your life. Now it's time to map out **how to get there**. Big visions can feel intimidating or abstract—this is where goal setting bridges the gap between dreams and reality. Think of your vision as a destination on a map. Your **goals** are the milestones along the road to reach that destination.

To ensure your goals actually move you toward your vision (and not off on a side track), they need to be meaningful and well-defined. This is where the classic SMART framework can help. SMART stands for **Specific, Measurable, Achievable, Relevant, and Time-bound**. It's a popular formula because it ensures your goals are clear and actionable. Let's break it down in simple terms:

- **Specific:** Target a precise outcome. A vague goal like "I want to get healthier" becomes specific when you say, "I will jog for 30 minutes, 5 days a week" or "I will lose 10 pounds in 3 months by eating clean and exercising." Specificity gives your goal a focus.

- **Measurable:** Quantify it or make it trackable. You should know unequivocally when you've achieved it. Instead of "be a better professional," a measurable goal might be "obtain my professional certification by December" or "get a promotion to Senior Analyst by Q4." Numbers, dates, or concrete criteria are your friends—they let you gauge progress.

- **Achievable:** Set goals ambitious enough to inspire you, but realistic enough that you can accomplish them with effort. If your vision is sky-high, break it into a goal that is within reach as a next step. For example, writing an entire novel in a month might not be achievable if you're new to writing, but completing the first three chapters in a month could be. Your goals should stretch you out of your comfort zone, without breaking you. (You can always set a new goal to build on successes—momentum is powerful.)

- **Relevant:** Align each goal with your *vision and values*. This is the heart of *meaningful* goal-setting. Ask yourself *"Why does this goal matter?"* If you can draw a line from the goal to your long-term vision or to something you deeply value, then it's relevant. For instance, setting a goal to save a certain amount of money makes sense if financial freedom or funding a future dream (like starting a business or buying a home) is part of your vision. If a goal doesn't clearly serve your vision, reconsider it—you have limited time and energy, so spend it on what counts.

- **Time-bound:** Every goal needs a target date or timeframe. A deadline creates a healthy sense of urgency and helps with planning. Open-ended goals can languish forever ("someday" is not a day of the week!). So add "...by [date]" to your goal statement. For example, "Learn conversational Spanish" becomes "Complete an intermediate Spanish course by October 30, 2025." Time-bound goals spur you to take action now and allow you to track progress over time.

TOOLKIT REFERENCE*To transform your vision into achievable goals, use the "SMART Goal Creation" and "Goal Alignment Check" exercises in Section 7 of the Practical Toolkit.*

Take your vision and identify a handful of **key long-term goals** (these might be 1-5 year goals) that would make that vision a reality. For example, if your vision includes running your own business, a long-term goal might be "Launch my online business and achieve sustainable income by 2027." If your vision includes being in excellent health, a long-term goal could be "Complete a marathon by 2024" or "Lose 50 pounds and reach 15% body fat within 2 years."

Make sure these goals meet the SMART criteria we discussed. Write them down—yes, **write them**. Studies show that simply writing down your goals dramatically increases the likelihood of achieving them. In fact, one study found people who wrote down their goals were **33% more successful** in reaching them than those who merely thought about their goals. There's power in putting pen to paper (or fingers to keyboard)—it turns a wish floating in your mind into a concrete commitment on the page.

"Goals are the stepping stones between your current reality and your envisioned future—place them strategically and cross them deliberately."

Once you have your big long-term goals, break each one into **smaller short-term goals or milestones**. This step is crucial: it's how you bring huge aspirations down into actionable pieces. Let's say one of your long-term goals is "earn a master's degree within 4 years." Short-term goals could be "apply to graduate programs by next March," "complete 3 courses in the first semester with a 3.5 GPA or higher," etc.

If the long-term goal is a marathon, a short-term goal might be "run a half-marathon within 12 months" or even "increase running distance from 2 miles to 6 miles over the next 3 months." Think of short-term goals as the **stepping stones** leading to the bigger goal. Achieving them gives you confidence and keeps you on track, while also providing opportunities to adjust your plan as needed.

It can also help to frame goals as **habits or actions** to take. For instance, if your long-term goal is to write a book, a relevant short-term goal might be "write 500 words daily for the next 90 days." Framing it this way makes it very concrete: either you wrote your 500 words today or you didn't—it's measurable daily.

Many successful people emphasize that consistent daily actions are what accomplish big goals over time. Jim Rohn taught that **"Success is nothing more than a few simple disciplines, practiced every day."** Those daily disciplines, modest on their own, compound into remarkable results. We'll talk more about daily actions in the next section, but as you set goals, consider linking them to regular routines: for example, a goal to deepen relationships could translate into a habit of calling one family member or friend every weekend, and so on.

Finally, ensure your list of goals isn't too overwhelming. It's better to have a focused set of truly meaningful goals than a laundry list of everything you've ever thought of doing. Think quality over quantity. If you achieve 3 major goals that transform your life, that's far better than partially achieving 10 miscellaneous ones. So prioritize: which goals will have the biggest impact on your life vision? Which excite you the most? Start with those. You can always revisit and add new goals once you've made headway on the initial ones. For now, pick a compelling few and let's get moving toward them.

Practical Exercise — From Vision to Goals: Look at the vision statement you wrote and identify 3–5 *major goals* that, when achieved, would signal you're living that vision. Write each goal as a SMART goal. For each one, list at least 1 short-term goal or milestone you need to hit along the way. For example:

- **Long-Term Goal (1 year):** *Earn a project management certification by June 2026 to advance my career.*

  ◦ *Milestone (3 months): Complete the required training course by March 2026.*

  ◦ *Milestone (6 months): Pass a full-length practice exam by May 2026.*

- **Long-Term Goal (2 years):** *Launch my side-business and make it profitable enough to quit my job by 2027.*

  ◦ *Milestone (1 month): Brainstorm and decide on a business niche and name.*

  ◦ *Milestone (3 months): Develop a basic product or service prototype.*

  ◦ *Milestone (6 months): Land first 5 paying customers.*

- **Long-Term Goal (6 months):** *Run a 10K race by next April (as a step toward my vision of an active, healthy lifestyle).*

  ◦ *Milestone (this week): Sign up for a 10K event to create accountability.*

  ◦ *Milestone (3 months): Be able to run 5K continuously (build up with a training plan).*

By sketching goals and milestones like this, you create a rough timeline for yourself. The next step will be aligning your **daily actions** to make sure these goals aren't just written down and forgotten, but actively pursued.

Figure 7.1: The Vision-to-Action Roadmap illustrates how your long-term vision connects to specific goals, which break down into actionable daily habits.

Aligning Daily Actions with Your Life Vision

Big goals set the direction, but *daily actions* determine your progress. This is where the rubber meets the road. It's empowering to declare a long-term goal like "Write a book in the next 12 months," but that goal will remain a daydream unless you translate it into what you need to do *today, tomorrow, and each week.* The secret to achieving your life vision is to **bridge the gap between the future and today's to-do list**. This means aligning your regular routines, habits, and choices with the goals you've set, so that each day—even in a small way—you are moving closer to your vision.

Think of your vision as the **summit of a mountain**. Your long-term goals are the base camps on the way up. Your short-term goals and habits are the daily steps, the climb itself. You can't jump straight to the peak; you reach it step by step, day by day. So ask yourself for each big goal: *"What's the next step I need to take?"* If your aim is to finish a degree, today's step might be "research 3 potential programs." If your aim is to get fitter, today's step might be "go for a 30-minute walk" or "prepare a healthy meal for dinner."

No action is too small—each one is like a brick laid in the foundation of your future. Consistency is far more important than grandeur here. As one proverb says, *"Little by little, a little becomes a lot."* The compound effect of modest but regular actions is enormous over time.

"The distance between your dreams and reality is measured in daily actions—close that gap one consistent step at a time."

TOOLKIT REFERENCE *To connect your vision to daily actions, practice the "Vision-to-Action Bridge" and "Daily Alignment Check" in Section 7 of the Practical Toolkit.*

One helpful practice is to **plan your weeks and days around your goals**. Many successful individuals do a weekly review (perhaps on Sunday evening) where they look at their goals and decide what key actions to schedule for the coming week. For example, if a goal is to write a certification exam, you might schedule study blocks on Monday, Wednesday, and Saturday. If a goal is to deepen your relationship with family, you might plan a family outing this weekend or set a reminder to call your parents mid-week.

By proactively slotting goal-aligned activities into your calendar, you ensure that urgent day-to-day busyness doesn't completely sweep aside your important long-term pursuits. It's all too easy to be *"busy but not productive"*—working hard all day but not on the things that truly matter to you. Intentional planning fixes that. Remember, **either you run the day or the day runs you**. Take charge of your schedule so that your daily life reflects your highest priorities.

Let's also talk about habits—those routine behaviors that make up a large part of our days. Harnessing habits is like putting parts of your goal pursuit on autopilot. Once a habit is ingrained, it doesn't take as much willpower to maintain, and it yields benefits repeatedly. Identify a few **key habits** that will drive you toward your vision. If your vision involves being a calm and centered person, a daily meditation habit could be transformative. If your vision involves professional growth, perhaps a habit of reading industry news each morning or practicing a skill for 20 minutes a day would help. Health vision? A habit of exercising at a set time or prepping healthy meals on Sundays could be game-changers.

These habits, small in themselves, become the engines of progress. Over time, they compound—much like how saving a little money regularly can grow into a large sum with interest. The difference between merely setting a goal and actually achieving it often comes down to the daily habits you build around that goal. To quote Jim Rohn again: **"Success is nothing more than a few simple disciplines, practiced every day."** By aligning your habits with your goals, you make success a daily process.

Practical Tip: Don't try to overhaul your entire life overnight. Focus on embedding *one or two new habits at a time*. Tie them to existing routines (for instance, "after I brew my morning coffee, I will spend 10 minutes reviewing my flashcards for class" or "after returning from my lunch break, I will take a 5-minute walk around the block"). These are sometimes called "habit stacking" or "anchor habits"—using an existing behavior as a cue for a new one. Over weeks, these goal-aligned actions will start to feel natural.

Another key to aligning daily actions is to continually remind yourself of your **vision and 'why'**. One technique is to keep visual cues in your environment. You might pin your written vision statement or a vision board (a collage of images representing your goals) somewhere you'll see it each day. Seeing a picture of that beach where you plan to open your café, or the marathon medal, or your family happily together—whatever symbolizes your goals—can trigger the motivation to do the hard work on days when you'd rather procrastinate. It reconnects you with the purpose behind the effort.

Finally, maintain flexibility. Aligning daily actions doesn't mean rigidly scheduling every hour or never having fun. Life is dynamic, and you're designing a **life**, not a prison schedule. It's important to leave room for rest, spontaneous opportunities, and the unexpected. The aim is not perfection; it's consistency and intentionality. If you miss a day or something disrupts your plans, don't beat yourself up (remember the earlier lessons on resilience and self-compassion). Simply get back on track the next day. The path to your vision will have twists and turns—what matters is that you keep orienting yourself toward that North Star and stepping forward.

Building Your Roadmap: At this point, you have your vision and a set of long and short-term goals. A helpful exercise is to consolidate these into a simple **goal roadmap**. This can be as straightforward as a list or table outlining your major goals, the milestones under each, and target dates. Some people like to draw this as a timeline on paper or use a digital tool—do whatever appeals to you.

The act of creating a roadmap helps you visualize the sequence of steps and how today's tasks connect to the big picture. It also becomes a handy reference you can look at each week to gauge progress. Here's one way to structure it:

- **Long-Term Goal** (1-5 years)

    ○ Milestone 1 (target date)

    ○ Milestone 2 (target date)

    ○ Milestone 3 (target date)

    ○ *Next Action:* (the very next step to take, e.g., "Call X for advice" or "research Y online")

Do this for each of your major goals. You'll end up with a master plan for designing your life. Remember, this plan isn't set in stone—it's a living document you will update as you learn and grow. But at any given moment, it gives you a sense of direction. As the saying goes, *"a goal without a plan is just a wish."* Now you have a plan. And each day, you'll execute pieces of it. By aligning what you do today with where you want to be tomorrow, you essentially start *living* your vision in advance. Your life gains a wonderful coherence—no part is wasted, because all parts are contributing to a greater whole.

TOOLKIT REFERENCE *To create your comprehensive life roadmap, use the "Master Goal Timeline" and "Next Action Identifier" tools in Section 7 of the Practical Toolkit.*

Sustaining Motivation Through Your "Why"

Setting goals and even developing good habits are tremendous steps, but maintaining the **motivation** to see them through is its own challenge. We're all enthusiastic when goals are new—think of the energy of New Year's resolutions. But inevitably, we hit obstacles or the initial excitement wears off. This is when many people quit... and when you will **not**, because you'll have something powerful on your side: a deep understanding of your **"why."**

Earlier we emphasized aligning goals to your values and purpose. That wasn't just a one-time exercise; it is the very thing that will keep your flame burning when the winds of adversity blow. As leadership expert Michael Hyatt put it, **"People lose their way when they lose their why."** If you stay connected to why each goal matters—truly matters—you will find the strength to persist.

Think back to *why* you set each of your major goals. What will achieving it bring to your life? How will it impact you or your loved ones or even the wider world? Maybe you want to advance in your career *to provide a better life for your family*, or *to make a bigger impact through your work*. Perhaps you seek better health *to have more years of joyful living* and *to be there for your children or grandchildren*. Maybe your goal is tied to a childhood dream that inspires your very soul.

These core reasons are your fuel. On the hard days, **remind yourself of your why**. One practical way is to write a short statement for each major goal: "I want to achieve _____ because _____." Keep these statements visible. For example: "I want to finish writing my novel because I have a story that could inspire others (and because becoming an author has been my dream since age 10)." On a day when writing feels tedious, reading that can reignite your commitment.

"When your 'why' is powerful enough, it transforms 'I should' into 'I must'—and that's when mountains move."

Another powerful technique to sustain motivation is to **visualize the outcome and the impact** regularly. Many top athletes and performers do this—they spend time vividly imagining the moment of success, *feeling* the emotions of it. You can do the same for your goals. Spend a few minutes in a quiet space, eyes closed, picturing yourself having achieved your goal. How do you feel? Proud, relieved, ecstatic? What are others saying to congratulate you? Imagine the benefits unfolding—for instance, if your goal was health-related, envision yourself hiking up a beautiful mountain, full of energy, something you couldn't do before.

This kind of visualization is not daydreaming; it's mental rehearsal. It makes the goal feel tangible and boosts your emotional drive to make it real. It's essentially a reminder of why it's worth it to push through today's discomfort.

Sample Future-Self Letter

One **immersive exercise** that combines visualization, emotional connection, and clarity is writing a **"future-self letter."** This is like sending a letter from the *you* five or ten years in the future, back to your present self. Below is a complete example of what such a letter might look like:

March 15, 2030

Dear [Your Name],

Greetings from the future! I'm writing to you from our home office, overlooking the garden we've cultivated over the years. The cherry trees are blooming, and I can hear our children playing outside with the dog we finally adopted last year.

First, I want you to know how proud I am of you—of us. The journey from where you are now to where I am today wasn't always smooth, but it was worth every step, every moment of doubt, and every obstacle we overcame.

Remember that business idea you're hesitating to pursue? The one that keeps you up at night with both excitement and fear? I'm happy to tell you we finally launched it nine months after you're reading this letter. The first year was challenging—we made mistakes, faced unexpected competition, and had to pivot our offering twice. But by year three, we had found our unique place in the market. Today, we employ twelve people who share our vision, and we've helped over 500 clients transform their lives.

That health goal you're working toward? Keep going. I'm writing to you 30 pounds lighter, with energy I haven't felt since college. Those morning walks you've been forcing yourself to take eventually became something I look forward to daily. In fact, last year we completed our first half-marathon! Remember how impossible that seemed? Trust me, your body is capable of more than you currently believe.

Our relationship with Mom has healed beautifully. Those weekly calls you started, even when conversations were awkward, gradually rebuilt the bridge between us. She was there for us during a difficult period two years from now, and that experience brought us closer than we've been since childhood.

Some advice from someone who knows you better than anyone:

1. Trust your instincts more. That gut feeling you often ignore? It's usually right.

2. The setbacks that are coming—and yes, there will be setbacks—are not failures. They're redirections toward something better.

3. Stop worrying so much about what others think. Five years from now, most of those opinions won't matter at all.

4. Take more risks creatively. Some of our most fulfilling projects came from ideas you're currently afraid might seem "too out there."

5. Spend more time in nature. The clarity and peace it brings is something we now consider essential.

When things get tough—and there will be days when you question everything—remember that I exist. I am real. This future is possible, and I'm living proof that you have what it takes to get here.

The path won't look exactly as you imagine it. Some doors will close unexpectedly, but better ones will open if you stay true to your purpose. The vision you're crafting now evolves over time, becoming richer and more fulfilling than you can currently envision.

Keep taking those small daily steps. Keep believing in yourself on the days when no one else seems to. Keep holding onto your 'why' when the 'how' seems impossible.

I'm waiting for you here in this future we've created, and I can't wait to see you arrive.

With love and confidence, [Your Future Self]

This letter, tucked away in your journal or saved in a special file, can serve as a powerful motivational anchor when challenges arise. Reading it reconnects you with the emotional reason behind your goals—the deeper purpose that transcends momentary difficulties.

TOOLKIT REFERENCE *To strengthen your motivational foundation, practice the "Deep Why Discovery" and "Future Self Letter" exercises in Section 7 of the Practical Toolkit.*

Now, even with a strong why and great visualization practices, motivation can still fluctuate. That's normal—we're human, not robots. So, build systems to **prop yourself up when motivation dips**. One system is **accountability**: share your goals with a trusted friend, mentor, or a group who will check in on your progress. When you know someone will ask "Hey, did you practice guitar this week like you said you would?", you're more likely to do it.

Accountability can also come in the form of joining a class or club related to your goal, or hiring a coach. It adds positive pressure and support. There's research indicating that having regular accountability check-ins can significantly increase your chances of success. Perhaps find a "goal buddy"—someone who is also working toward a goal—and agree to encourage each other and hold each other accountable with weekly updates.

Another system is to track and celebrate progress. Motivation isn't only about huge leaps; it grows when you acknowledge the small wins. Keep a simple log of efforts and improvements. Maybe you journal briefly each day about one thing you did that moved you forward. When you look back over a month, you'll be amazed at the accumulation of steps. And absolutely **celebrate milestones** when you hit them. Completed your 8-week workout program? Treat yourself to something (maybe new workout gear or a relaxing massage). Finished a draft of that book chapter? Celebrate with a nice dinner or a fun activity. These rewards reinforce your behavior and give you mini parties to look forward to, making the journey enjoyable. Success should feel good—allow yourself to feel proud along the way.

Even with all this, there will be tough times. Maybe you miss a goal deadline or face an unexpected setback. In those moments, remember the concept of *antifragility* we touched on earlier: the idea that obstacles can actually make you stronger. Instead of seeing a setback as proof you can't do this, reframe it as **training**. You're in the gym of life, and this challenge is just a way to build your resilience muscle.

Jim Rohn captured this mindset well: **"Don't wish it were easier, wish you were better... Don't wish for less challenge, wish for more wisdom."** Each challenge is teaching you something that will serve you on the road ahead. Maybe missing a self-imposed deadline teaches you to plan more conservatively next time, or that you needed to develop a particular skill first. Maybe an obstacle reveals a new passion or a better path. Stay flexible and **adapt** rather than quit. If one approach isn't working, tweak it.

If your goal truly matters to you (your "why" is strong), *there's always another way*. Sometimes your goals might even evolve—and that's okay. Keep the end vision in mind, but be open to changing the route.

One practical habit to maintain motivation and alignment is regular **self-assessment**. Set aside time, perhaps once a month, to review your progress on goals. Ask yourself: *What wins did I have? What challenges showed up? What did I learn?* This reflection turns every experience, good or bad, into growth. If you find your motivation waning for a particular goal, revisit your why or adjust the goal to make it more inspiring. Life is too short to pursue goals that don't ignite you—sometimes our priorities shift, and you might realize a goal you set isn't as relevant anymore. Give yourself permission to refine your plan.

The journey to your purpose is not a straight line. Think of it like sailing: you'll frequently need to tack—small course corrections—to stay on course toward your destination. That doesn't mean you're lost; it means you're actively navigating. Throughout this process, maintain a sense of *curiosity and kindness* toward yourself. Instead of harsh judgment, use missteps as feedback. You're learning how to live your best life—there's no manual for that, only persistence and self-awareness.

Above all, keep that **vision** in your sights. When motivation ebbs, reconnect with the future you're building. Read your vision statement again. Envision the faces of people who will benefit from you reaching your goals (maybe your children, students, customers, community members). This brings your endeavor out of your head and into the heart.

Passion lives in the heart. When you work from passion and purpose, you tap into a well of energy that is far more enduring than sheer willpower. Your deeper why is like a generator that keeps refueling your efforts, whereas surface-level motivation might just be like a single battery charge. Whenever you sense that generator sputtering, take time to service it—revisit purpose, adjust your mindset, lean on your support system—and you will find your drive restored.

Purpose Discovery Checklist

If you're still seeking clarity on your life's purpose, the following questions can help uncover what truly matters to you. Take your time with each one, listening for the quiet voice of authentic desire beneath the noise of external expectations:

What Brings You Joy?

- What activities make you lose track of time?

- What did you love doing as a child, before others told you what you "should" do?

- When was the last time you felt truly alive and engaged? What were you doing?

- What topics do you find yourself reading about or discussing with genuine interest?

What Are Your Natural Strengths?

- What comes easily to you that others find difficult?

- What kind of problems do people consistently come to you for help with?

- What have you been complimented on throughout your life?

- When have you felt most confident and capable?

What Matters To Your Heart?

- What injustices or problems in the world most disturb you?

- If you could solve one problem in your community, what would it be?

- What would you work on even if you never got paid or recognized for it?

- Whose lives do you most want to impact positively?

Legacy Questions

- At the end of your life, what would you want people to remember about you?

- What contribution do you want to have made to the world?

- What experiences would you regret not having?

- If you had unlimited resources, how would you spend your time?

Values Exploration

- What three values would you never compromise, even under pressure?

- When have you felt most proud of yourself? What values were you honoring?

- When have you felt ashamed or disappointed in yourself? What values were compromised?

- Who do you admire most, and what qualities in them do you value?

After reflecting on these questions, look for patterns in your answers. The intersection of what you love, what you're good at, what the world needs, and what resonates with your values often points toward your purpose. Remember that purpose isn't always a specific career or role—it can be a theme that expresses itself in various ways throughout your life.

Conclusion: The Beginning of Your Next Chapter

As we conclude this chapter on purpose and direction, remember that this isn't an *ending*—it's a **beginning**. You've assembled the pieces: clarified who you are and what you value, painted a vision of the life you want, set goals to make it happen, and begun aligning your daily life to move in that direction. In short, you've designed a roadmap for your future. But a roadmap is only useful if you embark on the journey. Now is the time to take that courageous first step forward.

It might be a small step—writing one paragraph of your book, signing up for a class, waking up an hour earlier to exercise, calling that friend to discuss a business idea—but it's a significant one. By taking action, you're answering the call of your own vision.

"The most profound act of self-creation happens when you translate your vision into that first, courageous action—everything after is simply following through."

Pause for a moment and acknowledge how far you've come. Many people never even dare to articulate their purpose or set long-term visions; many let life simply carry them along. But here you are, actively **designing your life**. That's something to be proud of. It means you believe in your potential and your worth. It means you are taking responsibility for your happiness and fulfillment. In doing so, you join the ranks of those who live deliberately and passionately.

Yes, there will be uncertainties ahead and undoubtedly some detours. But armed with your purpose and goals, you will never be truly lost—you have your North Star. On tough days, you can orient back to your vision and adjust your sails. On good days, you will feel the wind propelling you forward faster than you imagined.

Every step you take, no matter how small, is writing the next chapter of your life's story. You cannot accomplish everything overnight—major life changes take time—but as Jim Rohn said, **"You cannot change your destination overnight, but you can change your direction overnight."** Today, right now, you can change your direction toward your dreams. And once the direction is set, it's just a matter of continuing forward. Consistency and perseverance will perform what we often call "miracles" over time. Trust this process. There is magic in compound effort and in staying true to your *why*. Five years from now, you will thank yourself for the steps you begin taking today.

TOOLKIT REFERENCE *To solidify your commitment to your life design, complete the "Purpose Declaration" and "First Action Commitment" exercises in Section 7 of the Practical Toolkit.*

So here is your invitation: **Start**. However modestly, start. Review your vision and goals often—keep them fresh and alive. Take one concrete action in the next 24 hours that moves you a tiny bit closer to a key goal (make that phone call, draft that email, lace up those running shoes). Then plan another for tomorrow. In a year, you'll look back in astonishment at how these tiny steps add up to real transformation.

Embrace the journey with curiosity. There will be surprises—some welcome, some not—but all of them will shape you. You will grow in skills, yes, but also in character. The true reward of pursuing meaningful goals isn't just what you get, it's who you become. As Jim Rohn wisely noted, *"The major reason for setting a goal is for what it makes of you to accomplish it... what it makes of you will always be the far greater value than what you get."* By working diligently on your plan, you are in fact sculpting a stronger, wiser, more confident version of yourself. That is the ultimate prize.

Keep your mindset positive and resilient. If Plan A doesn't work out, remember that the alphabet has 25 more letters! Adjust and keep going, always aligned with your vision. Protect that vision like a precious seed—nurture it daily with your efforts and guard it from naysayers or momentary doubts. It's **your** vision; others might not see it or understand it, and that's fine. What matters is that *you* believe in it and are willing to work for it.

In closing, think of your life as a grand adventure—and you've just mapped out a thrilling new chapter. The world needs people living with purpose, people like you who have come alive with a mission. Your journey will not only uplift you, but also inspire those around you. So step forward with confidence and enthusiasm. The path ahead is yours to create, one day at a time. Keep your eyes on that North Star, keep your heart connected to your why, and know that you have everything inside you needed to reach that beautiful horizon you envisioned. This is just the beginning of an incredible voyage toward the life you were meant to live. **You've got this.** Now, go design a life you truly love—one purposeful step after another, all the way to your dreams.

Bridge to Chapter 8: From Design to Embodiment

As we transition from creating your life's blueprint to the final chapter of our journey together, we shift our focus from planning to living—from designing your path to embodying it fully. In Chapter 8, "Conclusion and Next Steps: Embodying Your New Identity," we'll explore how to integrate all you've learned into a sustainable, lifelong practice of growth.

The vision and purpose you've defined aren't just destinations—they represent the person you're becoming. Now it's time to fully step into that identity, to make your growth not just something you do but something you are. We'll discuss how to maintain momentum when the initial excitement fades, how to handle inevitable setbacks with grace, and how to continually refine your path as you evolve.

Think of it this way: if the previous chapters have been about building the vehicle for your journey and charting your course, the next chapter is about becoming a skilled driver who can navigate any terrain with confidence. You've laid the foundation, set the direction, and now you're ready to fully embody the transformed person who will make this vision a reality.

Let's complete our journey by discovering how to live as the person you've been working to become—not just for a season, but for a lifetime.

8

— ◆ —

CONCLUSION AND NEXT STEPS — EMBODYING YOUR NEW IDENTITY

The air is thin and crisp at the mountaintop. Our exhausted hiker gazes out at a golden horizon, heart pounding with a mix of triumph and humility. This moment feels like a rite of passage: the person who started at the foot of the mountain is not the same person who now stands at the peak. During the climb there were doubts, slips, and weary pauses, but also breakthroughs of confidence and strength. Each step upward was a step into a *new identity*—one forged through effort, insight, and resilience. Now, at the summit, our hiker breathes deeply and understands: they have *become* someone new. They have earned this view.

Imagine **you** are that hiker. In many ways, you are. Your "mountain" has been this journey of personal growth over the past chapters. You started at basecamp with a question: *who could I become if I really committed to change?* You gathered your gear—your values, your goals, your determination—and began the ascent.

Along the way, you stumbled on obstacles that tested your discipline and encountered storms that challenged your mindset. There were days you felt like quitting, but you didn't. Instead, you kept climbing, one lesson and one step at a time. And with each step, you shed old beliefs and excuses, gaining strength and wisdom. Now you've reached a kind of summit. **Congratulations on coming this far.** Take a moment to look back at the distance you covered. The very fact that you persisted to the end of this journey is proof of how much you've grown.

"The summit of personal growth isn't reaching perfection, but becoming someone who embraces the endless journey of becoming."

TOOLKIT REFERENCE*To capture your journey's insights, complete the "Personal Growth Milestone" reflection in Section 8 of the Practical Toolkit.*

A Lifelong Journey of Growth

This summit you've reached is not the end—it's a commencement, a fresh start. Personal development has no finish line; it's an ongoing adventure. The ancient sages and modern mentors agree on this fundamental truth: *"This business of personal development lasts a lifetime."* In other words, the journey of becoming your best self is a journey you'll be on for the rest of your days—and that's a beautiful thing. Every experience from here forward, whether a success or setback, is another trail on the mountain range of life. There's always a higher peak to climb, another level of understanding to reach.

Rather than being daunted by the fact that growth never ends, feel excited that **life will always offer new ways for you to learn, evolve, and shine.** Growth is a daily practice, a mindset, a lifestyle. You are now a *lifelong climber* on the mountain of self-improvement—stronger, wiser, and equipped with the tools to keep ascending.

Consider the story of Sara Blakely, founder of Spanx. Long after becoming a billionaire entrepreneur, she continued attending personal development seminars and reading growth-oriented books daily. When asked why she still invested in her growth despite her success, she explained, "The journey never ends. My father taught me that failure isn't the outcome—failure is not trying. Every day is another chance to grow stronger, wiser, and more capable than yesterday." This commitment to continuous growth, regardless of external success, exemplifies the lifelong climber mindset.

Of course, real life will continue to test you. There will be new challenges that arise next week, next year, five years from now. But now you know what to do when you face those tests. When life throws you an unexpected curveball, you won't see it as defeat—you'll see it as an *opportunity* to apply everything you've learned. Think of a skilled sailor: they can't control the wind, but they have mastered the art of adjusting their sails. You too have learned to adjust your sails.

"The true master isn't someone who never falls, but someone who uses every fall as a lesson in how to rise stronger."

Integrating Your Journey: The Seven Pillars

Let's take a moment to integrate the key lessons from each chapter of our journey together. These seven pillars now form the foundation of your continued growth:

1. Self-Awareness (Chapter 1: Know Yourself)

You've learned to face yourself honestly, without excuses or denial. This clarity about your strengths, weaknesses, and patterns is your starting point for all growth. Remember Marcus, who finally looked in the mirror and owned his part in his life's challenges? That honesty changed everything.

Integration Practice: Continue your self-reflection habit. Whether through journaling, meditation, or regular check-ins, maintain that honest dialogue with yourself. When facing a challenge, ask: "What is my part in this? What can I learn here?"

2. Values Alignment (Chapter 2: Building Your Compass)

You've identified your core values—the principles that guide your decisions and actions. This internal compass provides direction and stability in an ever-changing world. Like a lighthouse on a foggy shore, your values help you navigate when visibility is poor.

Integration Practice: Regularly check your decisions against your core values. Before making significant choices, ask: "Does this align with who I want to be?" When you feel uncertain, return to your compass—it will rarely steer you wrong.

TOOLKIT REFERENCE *To maintain integration of all seven pillars, complete the "Holistic Growth Review" worksheet in Section 8 of the Practical Toolkit.*

3. Disciplined Action (Chapter 3: Brick by Brick)

You've learned that consistent, disciplined action is the bridge between intention and reality. Remember Alex, who transformed his life by keeping small promises to himself? Those daily actions compounded into remarkable change.

Integration Practice: Continue building your "habit stack"—those small, daily disciplines that align with your goals. Remember the two-day rule: never skip a positive habit twice in a row. Focus on consistency over intensity.

4. Emotional Mastery (Chapter 4: Mastering the Inner Game)

You've developed tools to work with your thoughts and emotions rather than being controlled by them. Like Maya, you've learned to recognize negative thought patterns, practice self-compassion, and maintain perspective during emotional storms.

Integration Practice: Make mindfulness a daily habit. When emotions arise, name them, create space around them, and choose your response rather than reacting automatically. Remember that thoughts are not facts—they're mental events you can observe and question.

5. Physical Well-Being (Chapter 5: Physical Well-Being and Energy)

You've recognized that your physical body is the vehicle for your journey—and that sleep, nutrition, movement, and hydration form the foundation for all other growth. Physical vitality enhances every aspect of your development.

Integration Practice: Honor your body's needs. Maintain your sleep routine, stay hydrated, move daily, and fuel yourself well. These aren't "extra" priorities—they're the baseline that makes everything else possible.

6. Meaningful Connection (Chapter 6: The Power of Connection)

You've explored how to build and nurture relationships that support your growth while contributing to others' well-being. No meaningful journey happens in isolation, and your connections with others enrich your path.

Integration Practice: Invest in quality relationships. Practice deep listening, express appreciation, set healthy boundaries, and be fully present with others. Remember that connection is a fundamental human need—not a luxury.

7. Purpose and Direction (Chapter 7: Purpose and Direction)

You've learned to design a life of meaning and purpose, setting a course that reflects your authentic self and deepest aspirations. You've created a vision that pulls you forward and goals that map the path.

Integration Practice: Regularly revisit your life vision and check your progress on meaningful goals. Are your daily and weekly actions aligned with your larger purpose? Make adjustments as needed to stay on your chosen path.

"Integration is where knowledge becomes wisdom—when lessons from all parts of your journey merge into a cohesive whole that guides your every step."

Embodying Your Best Self

The greatest reward of this journey is not just having learned a list of concepts—it's the fact that you've integrated them into *who you are*. You are now living proof of the power of self-improvement. In Chapter 1, you became **self-aware** of your core values and beliefs; now, you're a person who acts in harmony with those values each day. In Chapter 2, you built your **compass**; now, when you set your mind to something, you follow through even when it's hard. In Chapter 3, you developed a resilient **mindset**; now, challenges that once rattled you are met with calm and confidence.

Think of your personal development as a mosaic, with each tile being one lesson or habit you've picked up. Individually, each piece is valuable, but together they form a beautiful, complete picture—the picture of **you, transformed**. You likely notice it in small, everyday moments: perhaps this morning you automatically practiced gratitude as you woke up, or you found it easy to choose a healthy breakfast because you value your wellness. At work, maybe you handled a stressful situation with a level head and solution-focused mindset that surprises even you. When talking with loved ones, you might be truly present and listening deeply, where before you might have been distracted or reactive.

These are the subtle yet profound indicators that you're *living* the change. It's not just theory in a book anymore—it's *you*. Where once you had to consciously remember to, say, pause and breathe when angry, now it happens almost naturally. Where once you had to push yourself to get up early and exercise, now it's simply part of your identity as a disciplined person. **This is integration**—all the growth you've worked for has become woven into the fabric of your life.

TOOLKIT REFERENCE *To deepen your embodiment of your best self, practice the "Identity Integration" visualization in Section 8 of the Practical Toolkit.*

Becoming Your Own Coach

Through this journey you had guidance (from this book, from mentors or teachers quoted, and from your own inner voice). Now, as you step into the next chapter of life, **you become your own coach**. The wisest, most motivated part of you—your "best self"—can be the voice that leads you onward. Continue the habits of reflection and self-correction that you developed here. When faced with a tough decision or a moment of indecision, pause and ask yourself: *What would the best version of me do right now?* Listen for that answer—it's in you.

As you practice self-coaching, remember that it's okay to stumble. Even the best coaches revise their strategies. When you catch yourself falling into a negative mindset or procrastinating on a goal, don't beat yourself up. Instead, treat it as your coach would: with honesty and encouragement. You might say to yourself, "Alright, I slipped up. What can I learn from this, and how do I get back on track?" By responding to yourself with accountability *and* compassion, you continue the cycle of growth.

"Being your own coach means combining the wisdom to know better with the compassion to do better—guiding yourself with firm kindness toward your highest potential."

While you coach yourself, you might also feel a natural urge to **pay it forward**—to help others on their journeys. One of the most beautiful parts of growth is that it creates a ripple effect. When others see you thriving and changing, they'll be curious how you did it. Some might even reach out and ask for advice or support. This is your chance to become a guide for someone else, even in small ways.

TOOLKIT REFERENCE

To develop your self-coaching practice, use the "Inner Coach Dialogue" and "Weekly Growth Review" techniques in Section 8 of the Practical Toolkit.

Handling External Resistance

As you embody your new identity and continue to grow, you may encounter a challenge many don't anticipate: resistance from others. Sometimes the people closest to us—family, friends, or colleagues—can be uncomfortable with our changes, even positive ones. This resistance isn't necessarily because they wish you ill; rather, your transformation disrupts the familiar dynamics they're accustomed to.

You might hear comments like, "You've changed," delivered not as a compliment but with confusion or concern. Or perhaps more subtle forms of resistance: eye rolls when you decline a drink because you're committed to your health, or dismissive remarks about your new morning routine or boundaries.

Remember three important truths when facing this resistance:

1. **Your growth is not a criticism of others.** Sometimes people interpret your changes as an implicit judgment of their choices. Reassure them that your path is personal—not a statement about theirs.

2. **True relationships can evolve.** The healthiest connections will adjust and potentially even strengthen as you grow. Some relationships may require renegotiation of their terms; a few might naturally fade. This is normal and okay.

3. **Consistency speaks louder than explanations.** You don't need to defend or over-explain your growth. Simply living your truth consistently will eventually earn respect, even from initial skeptics. As Jim Rohn wisely observed, "Let your actions speak so loudly that others cannot hear what you say."

The most powerful response to external resistance is internal certainty. When you're firmly anchored in your values and vision, others' doubts may create momentary waves, but they cannot divert your course. Stay steadfast, remain kind, and let the evidence of your transformation eventually speak for itself.

Your Continuous Growth Plan: Practical Next Steps

Growth without a plan often stalls. To maintain your momentum and continue evolving, consider these practical next steps:

1. Create a Personal Growth Ritual

Establish a regular time (daily, weekly, or monthly) dedicated to your ongoing development. This might include:

- A daily morning practice (journaling, meditation, reviewing your values and goals)

- A weekly review (reflecting on lessons learned, celebrating wins, setting intentions for the week ahead)

- A monthly deeper dive (assessing progress on larger goals, adjusting your approach as needed)

This structured approach creates a rhythm for your continued growth, ensuring it doesn't get lost in daily busyness.

2. Build Your Growth Environment

Your environment shapes your behavior more than willpower alone. Set yourself up for success by:

- Creating physical spaces that support your growth (a meditation corner, a workout area, a distraction-free workspace)

- Curating your digital environment (limiting notifications, following accounts that inspire you, using apps that support your goals)

- Surrounding yourself with growth-minded people (joining communities, establishing accountability partnerships)

Remember: what surrounds you, influences you. Design your environment to make growth the path of least resistance.

3. Develop a Learning Practice

Continuous growth requires continuous learning. Commit to:

- Reading regularly (books, articles, research in areas that interest you)

- Seeking diverse perspectives (people with different backgrounds, contrasting viewpoints)

- Applying what you learn (experiments, skill practice, teaching others)

The goal isn't just to accumulate knowledge but to integrate it into your life through application.

"Learning without application is merely entertainment—it's in the doing that knowledge transforms into wisdom."

4. Establish Review and Renewal Points

Set specific times to take stock of your journey and renew your commitment:

- Quarterly reviews (What's working? What needs adjustment? What have I learned?)

- Annual reflection (How have I grown this year? What do I want to focus on next?)

- Life transition points (How do major changes affect my path? What new growth opportunities do they present?)

These checkpoints prevent drift and ensure your growth remains intentional rather than accidental.

5. Create Your Continued Growth Curriculum

Based on your reflection, identify your next areas of growth:

- Skills to develop (technical, interpersonal, creative)

- Qualities to strengthen (patience, courage, resilience)

- Experiences to seek (challenges, exposure to new environments)

View yourself as a lifelong student with a personalized curriculum that evolves as you do.

TOOLKIT REFERENCE *To implement your continuous growth plan, use the "Ongoing Growth Blueprint" template in Section 8 of the Practical Toolkit.*

9

———— • ————

PRACTICAL PHILOSOPHY & PSYCHOLOGY TOOLKIT

Introduction

This toolkit brings together powerful techniques from ancient philosophy, modern psychology, and evidence-based practices to help you navigate life's challenges with greater clarity and resilience. Each tool is presented with its origin, a concise description, and a practical real-world example so you can apply it immediately in your daily life.

Whether you're facing difficult emotions, making tough decisions, dealing with anxiety, overcoming depression, building resilience, seeking purpose, developing your identity, or establishing positive habits, you'll find practical techniques to help. These tools have stood the test of time and scientific scrutiny.

How to Use This Guide: Browse through the sections relevant to your current needs, or work through the entire toolkit systematically. Try implementing one or two techniques at a time, practicing them consistently before adding more to your repertoire. Remember that these are skills that improve with practice.

Table of Contents

1. Emotional Regulation Tools

2. Decision-Making & Clarity Tools

3. Anxiety & Stress Management Tools

4. Depression & Meaning Tools

5. Resilience & Adversity Tools

6. Purpose & Self-Identity Tools

7. Discipline & Habits Tools

Emotional Regulation Tools

These techniques help you manage intense emotions, respond rather than react, and maintain emotional balance in challenging situations. Use them when you notice yourself becoming angry, anxious, frustrated, or overwhelmed.

Dichotomy of Control

Origin: Stoicism (Epictetus)**Description:** Focus on what's within your control and release attachment to what isn't. Epictetus taught that we control our opinions, choices, and reactions, but not external events.**Real-world Use:** Next time you feel anxious about a job outcome, list what you **can control** (preparing, effort) and what you **cannot** (hiring decisions). Act on the controllables and mentally dismiss the uncontrollables, reducing worry about things beyond your influence.

Negative Visualization

Origin: Stoicism (Seneca, Epictetus)**Description:** Envision worst-case scenarios to build resilience and foster gratitude. Also known as *premeditatio malorum*.**Real-world Use:** Each morning, picture a challenge (e.g., a tough meeting) going poorly. Accept that possibility, then proceed calmly knowing you can handle it. This reduces anxiety over "what ifs" by training your mind to face fears rather than avoid them.

Objective Description

Origin: Stoicism (Epictetus, Marcus Aurelius)**Description:** Describe events in purely factual, non-emotional language to avoid emotional escalation.**Real-world Use:** Instead of yelling, "What a jerk!" when cut off in traffic, calmly note, "Another driver moved his car in front of mine, slowing my progress slightly." This logical reframing quickly bypasses anger.

Emotion Labeling

Origin: Neuroscience, mindfulness**Description:** Explicitly naming an emotion reduces its intensity and engages rational brain centers.**Real-world Use:** When anxious before speaking publicly, mentally state, "I'm feeling anxiety right now." This labeling activates calming neural pathways, reducing emotional intensity.

Cognitive Distancing

Origin: Stoicism & CBT (Epictetus, Beck)**Description:** Question harmful thoughts rather than accepting them as truth. Remember "People are not disturbed by things, but by their views of things."**Real-world Use:** When gripped by anger or anxiety, write down the triggering thought. Ask: "Is this entirely true? What might I be overlooking?" By treating thoughts as opinions rather than facts, you can reframe negativity and calm the emotional storm.

The View from Above

Origin: Stoicism (Marcus Aurelius)**Description:** Adopt a bird's-eye perspective to reduce emotional overwhelm.**Real-world Use:** When stressed by a personal setback, visualize looking down at your life from space. Notice how small the issue is relative to the world's vastness. This helps replace panic with calm, as you realize many worries are minor in the big picture.

Delay & Breath (Anger Management)

Origin: Stoicism (Seneca)**Description:** Pause before reacting in anger. As Seneca advised, "The greatest remedy for anger is delay."**Real-world Use:** The next time something infuriating happens, stop and take a few slow breaths. This short circuit gives your rational mind a chance to kick in, preventing hasty reactions. After the pause, respond calmly or decide it's not worth responding at all.

4-7-8 Breathing

Origin: Yoga Pranayama (adopted in modern stress relief)**Description:** Using slow, controlled breathing patterns to signal your body to relax.**Real-world Use:** When you feel anger or panic rising, inhale deeply for 4 seconds, hold for 7 seconds, then exhale for 8 seconds. Repeat a few times. This slows your heart rate and helps your intense emotions subside.

Pushbutton Technique

Origin: Adlerian Psychology (Alfred Adler)**Description:** Shift your emotional state by recalling vivid memories.**Real-world Use:** When feeling down or angry, intentionally "press the positive button." Close your eyes and relive a happy moment with as much detail as possible. Notice the warm emotions returning. This reminds you that by changing what you dwell on, you can lift your mood on demand.

Stoic Journaling (Evening Reflection)

Origin: Stoicism (Seneca, Marcus Aurelius)**Description:** Review your day each night to regulate emotions and improve behavior.**Real-world Use:** Before bed, write brief answers to: "What did I do today? What did I do well? What could I do better?" Be objective and gentle – this is self-improvement, not self-blame. Regular evening review builds emotional awareness and reinforces progress.

The Iceberg Analogy

Origin: Psychology (Gottman Institute)**Description:** Recognize anger's hidden sources. Like an iceberg, visible anger is just the tip, with hidden emotions (hurt, fear, stress) underneath.**Real-world Use:** Next time you're angry, ask: "What's beneath this anger?" Maybe you're hurt by a comment or afraid of losing respect. By naming the core feeling ("I'm hurt"), you can address the true issue instead of exploding in anger.

Unconditional Positive Regard (UPR)

Origin: Humanistic Psychology (Carl Rogers)**Description:** Practice total acceptance (first with yourself, then with others).**Real-world Use:** When self-criticism or shame arises, speak to yourself as a supportive friend: "I accept you. You are more than this slip-up." This self-compassion reduces harsh emotions like guilt and anxiety, creating an emotionally safe environment for both you and those around you.

Decision-Making & Clarity Tools

These techniques help you make better choices, overcome indecision, and gain mental clarity. They're especially useful when facing important decisions, feeling stuck, or needing to cut through mental fog.

The Golden Mean

Origin: Classical Philosophy (Aristotle)**Description:** Aim for the virtuous middle ground between extremes.**Real-world Use:** When facing a decision, identify the extremes: too little vs. too much. If you're considering giving feedback: too little honesty (avoidance) vs. too much bluntness (cruelty). Then aim for the moderate approach – honest yet kind feedback. Using the Golden Mean helps you make balanced decisions.

Socratic Questioning

Origin: Classical Philosophy (Socrates) via modern CBT**Description:** Probe assumptions to clarify thinking by asking systematic questions.**Real-world Use:** If you're stuck on a decision like "I must pick the perfect career or I'll fail," Socratically challenge it: "What does 'fail' mean? Is one choice really everything? Who says I can't change later?" Writing out these Q&As often reveals a more nuanced view, clearing up mental fog and allowing wiser, less fear-driven decisions.

Enchiridion's Maxim

Origin: Stoicism (Epictetus)**Description:** Remember that events themselves are neutral – your judgment shapes the outcome.**Real-world Use:** When a project fails, instead of "This is a disaster," tell yourself, "This is tough, but what can I learn?" By viewing the setback as feedback for growth, you'll decide your next steps more rationally. This tool turns emotional reactions into calm evaluation, improving choices under pressure.

Pros vs. Cons with Values

Origin: Modern Psychology (Decision Analysis)**Description:** Weigh decisions by listing pros/cons, then factor in your core values.**Real-world Use:** If deciding whether to switch jobs, list practical pros (higher pay, new skills) and cons (uncertain stability, moving). Then list your top values (e.g., family time, growth, security). See which option honors those values. This structured reflection guides you to a decision that you'll feel at peace with.

10-10-10 Rule

Origin: Modern Strategy (Suzy Welch)**Description:** Consider how you'll feel about a decision in 10 minutes, 10 months, and 10 years.**Real-world Use:** If you're torn about making a big purchase, apply 10-10-10: How will I feel about this in 10 minutes (excited, guilty?), in 10 months (still happy I have it or regretting the cost?), and in 10 years (will it matter then?). This time perspective can reveal whether the choice is truly right for you.

Eternal Recurrence Test

Origin: Existential Philosophy (Friedrich Nietzsche)**Description:** Choose as if you had to live this life choice on repeat forever.**Real-world Use:** When torn about a big life decision (career change, moving city), imagine repeating your current life eternally. Does staying in your current path forever excite or depress you? If the idea of making a change feels daunting but worth an eternity, that signals it aligns with your authentic desires.

Acting As If

Origin: Adlerian Psychology (Alfred Adler)**Description:** Make decisions by briefly acting as the person you aspire to be.**Real-world Use:** If you're indecisive because of self-doubt (e.g., whether to take a leadership role), for one day act as if you are already a confident leader. Dress the part, make decisions decisively, and speak up in meetings. This gives experiential evidence to inform your decision, shifting perspective from "Can I?" to "How would I?"

The Stakeholder Chair

Origin: Modern Adaptation (inspired by Six Thinking Hats & Role-Play)**Description:** View a decision from multiple viewpoints by role-playing different stakeholders. **Real-world Use:** If deciding something that affects others, mentally "sit" in each person's chair. For a workplace policy, first take the employee's perspective: How does this affect their daily work? Next, the manager's chair: Does this improve performance? Finally, the customer's chair: Does this add value? This 360° understanding leads to decisions that are more well-rounded.

Cost of Inaction

Origin: Modern Psychology (Motivational interviewing concept)**Description:** When stuck, consider the pain of not deciding.**Real-world Use:** If you're procrastinating on a decision like starting therapy or a fitness regimen, list the costs of doing nothing. Staying the same could mean continued stress, poorer health, or regret. Highlighting these hidden costs can spur you to choose an option rather than drift.

Pre-Mortem Analysis

Origin: Modern Psychology (Gary Klein, also echoes Stoicism)**Description:** Imagine a future where your decision failed, and figure out why.**Real-world Use:** Before finalizing a big plan (launching a business, making an investment), do a pre-mortem. Write, "The project flopped because..." and brainstorm causes. This creative pessimism surfaces blind spots so you can address them proactively, making your decision more robust.

Third-Person Self-Talk

Origin: Modern Psychology (Self-distancing research)**Description:** Decide as if advising a friend, using your name.**Real-world Use:** When you have to make a tough personal decision, talk it out saying your name, e.g., "What should Alex do in this situation?" This creates a slight distance, allowing you to tap into your wiser, objective counsel. You'll often see the path that aligns with your principles more clearly.

Anxiety & Stress Management Tools

These techniques help reduce anxiety, manage stress, and create a sense of calm. Use them when feeling overwhelmed, facing uncertainty, or experiencing persistent worry or panic.

Stoic Acceptance (Amor Fati)

Origin: Stoicism/Existentialism (Marcus Aurelius, Nietzsche)**Description:** Love your fate – embrace reality instead of fighting it.**Real-world Use:** When feeling anxious about a situation you can't change (a delayed flight, lost job opportunity), repeat to yourself: "Amor fati – love this fate." Instead of "Why me?", say "What can I do with this?" This transforms anxiety into acceptance and proactive coping.

Worry Scheduling

Origin: Cognitive Behavioral Therapy**Description:** Limit worry to a set "worry period" each day.**Real-world Use:** Set a daily alarm (e.g., 7:00 pm) as "worry time." When anxious thoughts arise at 3:00 pm, jot them down and tell yourself, "I'll worry about this at 7." Continue your day. At 7:00, spend 15 minutes addressing the list. This tool trains your mind that you're in control of when and how to worry.

Progressive Muscle Relaxation (PMR)

Origin: Clinical Psychology (Edmund Jacobson)**Description:** Release anxiety by systematically tensing and relaxing the body.**Real-world Use:** When anxious before a presentation or to unwind at night, sit or lie down. Start at your feet: curl your toes hard...hold... then relax. Calves next: tighten...hold...relax. Continue up through thighs, abdomen, hands, arms, shoulders, face. This process lowers physical tension, sending a calm signal to your brain.

Box Breathing

Origin: Mindfulness/US Navy SEALs**Description:** Use structured breathing to quell anxiety.**Real-world Use:** Anytime panic or overwhelm strikes, discreetly do a few rounds of box breathing. Inhale for 4 seconds, hold for 4, exhale for 4, hold for 4 (like drawing a square). This steady pattern slows your heart rate and stabilizes cortisol, making your body feel safe. You can do this anywhere without anyone noticing.

Grounding Exercise (5-4-3-2-1)

Origin: Anxiety Management Technique (Modern Psychology)**Description:** Reconnect with the present moment through your five senses to break the cycle of anxious thoughts.**Real-world Use:** When panic rises, mentally note 5 things you see, 4 things you feel (touch), 3 things you hear, 2 things you smell, and 1 thing you taste. This sensory exercise pulls you out of your racing mind and back into the here-and-now, making anxiety more manageable.

Exposure Ladder

Origin: Cognitive Behavioral Therapy (Gradual exposure therapy)**Description:** Face fears step-by-step to reduce anxiety sensitivity.**Real-world Use:** If social anxiety makes you fear networking, your ladder might be: 1) Smile at a stranger and say hello; 2) Ask a coworker one question about their weekend; 3) Attend a casual meetup, stay 15 minutes; 4) Attend a larger event, chat with 2 people. Start at step 1, repeating until anxiety lessens, then move up.

Thought Labeling (Mindfulness)

Origin: Meditation practice**Description:** Detach from anxious thoughts by giving them labels.**Real-world Use:** During anxious moments, mentally step back and observe your thoughts like passing clouds. Label them: "planning thought," "catastrophizing thought," "self-criticism." This slight shift – treating the worry as an object, not a truth – diminishes its power. You realize you are not the anxiety; it's just an event in the mind.

Tragic Optimism

Origin: Existential Psychology (Viktor Frankl)**Description:** Find meaning in the midst of anxiety or crisis.**Real-world Use:** When anxiety peaks due to a serious life problem (job loss, illness), practice tragic optimism: ask, "What seed of meaning can I find here?" Maybe it's an opportunity to reconnect with loved ones, to learn resilience, or to help others in similar situations. This gives your pain a direction, making anxiety more manageable.

Challenge Catastrophic Thoughts

Origin: Cognitive Behavioral Therapy**Description:** Question the scary "what if" thoughts that fuel anxiety to see if they're exaggerated or likely.**Real-world Use:** If you start thinking, "What if I embarrass myself in this meeting and lose my job?" challenge it: "Has that ever happened? What's more likely is I might stumble on a word, and that's okay." By fact-checking your fears and considering realistic outcomes, you can defuse the anxiety they cause.

Worry Journaling & Trash

Origin: Therapeutic writing**Description:** Write out your anxieties, then literally throw them away.**Real-world Use:** When a looping worry keeps you up at night, grab a piece of paper and dump every anxious thought onto it unfiltered. Then crumple it up and toss it (or burn it safely). The brain often relaxes once it sees the concerns captured on paper, and the physical act of trashing them adds ritual closure.

Micro-Meditations

Origin: Buddhist psychology, Jon Kabat-Zinn**Description:** Brief, 30-60 second meditation pauses throughout your day to reset your emotional baseline.**Real-world Use:** Before entering a meeting, pause for 60 seconds. Breathe deeply and focus on sensations, centering yourself to enter calmly and intentionally.

Moral Inventory

Origin: Existential/Stoic – Seneca's conscience, 12-step influenced**Description:** Ease anxiety by checking your conscience and making amends.**Real-world Use:** If you feel uneasy and suspect it's guilt-based (maybe you snapped at a friend or cut a corner), do a quick moral inventory. Ask: "Is there something I've done or not done that's weighing on me?" If yes, plan one action to address it. Clearing these moral debts often lightens an emotional burden you didn't realize you were carrying.

Depression & Meaning Tools

These techniques help lift mood, find meaning in difficult circumstances, and rebuild motivation. They're particularly helpful when feeling hopeless, empty, or like life has lost its purpose.

Behavioral Activation

Origin: Clinical Psychology (Lewinsohn)**Description:** Do small enjoyable or meaningful activities to lift mood.**Real-world Use:** Make a weekly list of simple activities that you used to enjoy or find important (walking in the park, calling a friend, cooking a meal). Each day, push yourself to do at least one, even if you don't feel motivated. These actions often produce a spark of positive emotion that can start to snowball.

Cognitive Reframing

Origin: Cognitive Behavioral Therapy (Aaron Beck)**Description:** Identify and challenge depressive thoughts.**Real-world Use:** When you notice a heavy thought, write it down and label the distortion if you can. Then write a balanced counter-thought. If "I screwed up that presentation; I'm a total failure" is the thought, challenge it: "One presentation went poorly. I've done well before and can learn from this. One setback doesn't make me a failure."

Gratitude Journaling

Origin: Positive Psychology (Emmons, Seligman)**Description:** Counter depression by noting things you're grateful for.**Real-world Use:** Each evening, jot 3 things you're grateful for or that went well, no matter how small. On tough days, it might be as basic as "I had a warm bed." Over weeks, this practice increases mood and optimism by highlighting that even in dark times, there are glimmers of light.

Finding Your Why

Origin: Existential Psychology (Viktor Frankl)**Description:** Articulate a purpose or meaning that gives you reason to push through.**Real-world Use:** Sit down and complete the sentence: "My life is meaningful because __," or "Things I still want to do/give are __." Depression often makes life feel meaningless; actively defining a why acts like a north star, giving even small daily actions a sense of purpose.

Mastery Experiences

Origin: Psychology (Albert Bandura's self-efficacy)**Description:** Do things that make you feel competent, however minor.**Real-world Use:** Set a tiny goal each day that you know you can accomplish. It could be making your bed, watering a plant, or completing a short workout. When done, consciously acknowledge it: "I set out to do this, and I did it." Each success counters the thought "I can't do anything."

Social Connection Routine

Origin: Humanistic/Behavioral Psychology**Description:** Schedule regular contact with supportive people.**Real-world Use:** Make it a rule: every X days, reach out to someone – a quick text, a call, or coffee. Use structure: e.g., "Tuesdays = lunch with a coworker; Saturdays = call my cousin." Treat it like taking medicine, going through the motions even when you don't feel like it. Often, after or during the interaction, there's at least a slight uplift.

Self-Compassion Break

Origin: Buddhist Psychology (Kristin Neff's adaptation)**Description:** Treat yourself with kindness in moments of pain, as you would a dear friend.**Real-world Use:** When you notice you're mentally beating yourself up, pause. Take a deep breath and say to yourself: 1) "This is a moment of suffering." (acknowledge the pain); 2) "Suffering is a part of being human." (you're not alone); 3) "May I be kind to myself in this moment." Then offer kindness: perhaps place a hand on your heart or say something soothing.

"Not Worthy of My Suffering" Reframe

Origin: Existential Philosophy (Dostoevsky via Frankl)**Description:** Aim to respond to hardship in a way that honors your struggle.**Real-world Use:** When enduring depression, consider it a kind of "assignment" life has given you. Ask: "What response would make me worthy of this challenge? What action would dignify this pain?" By striving to be "worthy" of even the worst times, you create a narrative where you are the hero persevering, not just a victim.

Physical Exercise

Origin: Health Psychology**Description:** Using movement to boost mood, since exercise releases endorphins and can improve sleep and self-esteem.**Real-world Use:** You don't need to run a marathon – if you're depressed, even gentle exercise helps. Try doing 5 minutes of stretching or walking to the mailbox and back. Regular physical activity often improves mood and energy over time, functioning like a natural antidepressant.

Expressive Journaling

Origin: Therapeutic Writing**Description:** Writing freely about your feelings and thoughts as a way to process pain and release pent-up emotions.**Real-world Use:** When sadness or numbness feels overwhelming, grab a pen and paper and pour out whatever is on your mind for 10 minutes. You might start with "I feel..." The goal is to unburden yourself. Often you'll feel a bit lighter or clearer-headed after writing, as if you've talked it out with someone.

Professional Help & Support Plan

Origin: Pragmatic evidence-based approach**Description:** Recognize when depression isn't just sadness and have a plan for help.**Real-world Use:** If you notice persistent low mood, loss of interest, or hopelessness lasting more than two weeks, activate a support plan. This might include: researching therapists, talking to a doctor about options, or confiding in a trusted friend. Write down emergency steps for severe moments (like crisis line numbers). Getting professional help is not weakness – it's using all available tools.

Resilience & Adversity Tools

These techniques help you bounce back from setbacks, adapt to difficulties, and grow stronger through challenges. They're valuable when facing failure, loss, or any significant life disruption.

Antifragility Mindset

Origin: Modern Philosophy (Nassim Taleb, echoes Nietzsche)**Description:** See stress and trials as things that make you stronger, not weaker.**Real-world Use:** Next time you face a hardship (job loss, breakup, big mistake), deliberately frame it as "This is training." Ask: "How might this adversity actually benefit me in the long run?" By treating challenges as fuel for development, you adopt a survivor's mindset and bounce back quicker.

Obstacle → Opportunity (Marcus's "Obstacle is the Way")

Origin: Stoicism (Marcus Aurelius)**Description:** Turn obstacles upside down – every blockage is an opportunity in disguise.**Real-world Use:** When something goes wrong, immediately ask: "How can this be for me rather than against me?" If a project at work implodes, maybe it's an opportunity to showcase leadership by fixing it. Write the obstacle on paper, then arrow to a potential benefit: "X happened → which led me to Y (positive thing)."

Gratitude in Adversity

Origin: Stoicism (Seneca, modern research)**Description:** List reasons to be grateful especially when things go wrong.**Real-world Use:** When you're in a tough spot, force yourself to find 3 things that don't suck at that moment. Your car broke down? 1) I'm grateful I have a phone to call for help; 2) I'm safe and not hurt; 3) This might be a good story later. By shifting focus from 100% negativity to at least a 90/10 view, you inject hope and reduce the feeling of being cursed.

Growth Mindset

Origin: Developmental Psychology (Carol Dweck)**Description:** Believing that abilities and situations can improve with effort and learning.**Real-world Use:** After a setback like not getting a promotion, tell yourself, "I can grow from this." Ask, "What can I learn or do better for next time?" Instead of labeling yourself a failure, you view the experience as feedback. This attitude keeps you motivated to try again rather than giving up.

Humor as Armor

Origin: Psychology (defense mechanism, used by Frankl)**Description:** Use humor to lighten heavy situations.**Real-world Use:** Challenge yourself to find appropriate humor in a frustrating situation. Stuck in the hospital? Playfully rank the terrible cafeteria food like you're a food critic. By injecting silliness or wit, you momentarily flip your perspective from victim to observer/comedian, releasing tension and creating a mental buffer.

Role Model Resilience

Origin: Stoicism (Seneca's "ideal man", Modern – mentorship)**Description:** Imagine how your hero would handle this, and imitate.**Real-world Use:** Identify a person you admire for their toughness or grace under pressure. When you're in a difficult situation, ask yourself: "What would [Role Model] do or say right now?" By channeling their qualities, you momentarily step outside your own doubt or pain and adopt a more resilient stance.

Self-Distancing in Struggle

Origin: Modern Psychology (self-distancing techniques)**Description:** View your life like a movie where you are the hero overcoming the low point.**Real-world Use:** In a moment of hardship, imagine narrating your situation in the third person or picturing it on a screen. This mental trick makes you the protagonist of a story rather than a victim of chaos. It reminds you that in almost every great story, the hero hits a low before triumph.

Past Victories Log

Origin: Coaching Psychology**Description:** A personal list of challenges you've overcome or achievements you've made, used as a reminder of your strength and capability. **Real-world Use:** When you feel defeated, review a notebook or file where you've written things like "Graduated college against the odds," "Resolved a major conflict at work," or

"Recovered from surgery." This log proves to you that you've been resilient before, and can be again.

Learned Resourcefulness (Past Victories)

Origin: Psychology (Adaptive resilience)**Description:** Recall times you overcame challenges to remind yourself of your capabilities.**Real-world Use:** When facing a new adversity, spend a few minutes writing or thinking about at least two difficulties you've conquered in the past. Detail what the challenge was and how you dealt with it. By revisiting these triumphs, you activate a memory of resilience. "If I managed that, I can manage this."

Incremental Improvement (Kaizen)

Origin: Japanese philosophy of continuous improvement**Description:** In hard times, aim to get 1% better or make one aspect better.**Real-world Use:** Identify one small thing you can improve about the situation or yourself today. If you're recovering from surgery and bedridden, maybe you can do a simple breathing exercise to strengthen lungs. The mindset is: No matter how bad it is, I can likely make one thing slightly better. Celebrate that tiny win, then tomorrow find another.

Acceptance Commitment (ACT): "Clean vs. Dirty Pain"

Origin: Acceptance and Commitment Therapy**Description:** Accept inevitable pain but drop the extra suffering we add.**Real-world Use:** When something bad happens, acknowledge the clean pain: "Yes, this hurts." Allow yourself to feel it. But watch for the dirty pain thoughts. The moment you catch yourself ruminating "Why me? This ruins everything.", label it: "Okay, my mind is adding extra on top of the pain." Gently practice letting those thoughts go. Refocus on "What's within my control now?"

Active Problem-Solving

Origin: Cognitive Psychology (Problem-Focused Coping)**Description:** Tackling the controllable parts of a problem head-on, which restores a sense of agency and progress .**Real-world Use:** If your apartment floods and damages a lot of belongings, it's easy to feel overwhelmed. An active problem-solving approach is to break it down: call insurance, make a list of ruined items, see what can be saved, and start the cleanup one step at a time. By focusing on actionable steps, you feel less helpless and more empowered amid the chaos.

Purpose & Self-Identity Tools

These techniques help you discover meaning, clarify your values, and develop a stronger sense of who you are. They're useful when feeling directionless, experiencing an identity crisis, or seeking greater authenticity.

Ikigai — Four Pillars of Purpose

Origin: Japanese Philosophy**Description:** Find the intersection of what you love, what you're good at, what the world needs, and what can support you.**Real-world Use:** Draw four circles overlapping (a Venn diagram). Label them: Passion (what you love), Vocation (what you can be paid for), Profession (what you're good at), and Mission (what the world needs). Brainstorm elements for each circle from your life. See where they overlap to generate a purpose statement or next step.

Find Your "Why"

Origin: Existential Psychology (Viktor Frankl)**Description:** Defining the core purpose or mission that gives your life meaning, the "why" that drives you through challenges.**Real-world Use:** Take time to ask yourself, "What do I most want to contribute or accomplish in my life?" or "What pain or problem do I feel driven to help with?" Maybe it's creating beautiful art, helping others heal, or providing for your family. Write down your thoughts. When times get tough, reconnecting with this why reminds you why your efforts matter.

Values Clarification

Origin: Humanistic Psychology (Rollo May, Acceptance & Commitment Therapy)**Description:** Identify your core values and use them as a compass.**Real-world Use:** Take 10 minutes to list out values (words or short phrases that resonate). Circle your top 5. Now define what each means to you in behavioral terms. Keep this list visible. When you face a choice or feel adrift, consult it: "Which option aligns with my values? Have I neglected any values lately?"

Memento Mori

Origin: Stoicism (Epictetus, Marcus Aurelius)**Description:** Remember your mortality to stay grounded and prioritize what truly matters.**Real-world Use:** Wear a memento mori reminder (e.g., a ring or phone wallpaper) or spend a minute daily reflecting: "If today were my last, would this stress matter?" This perspective reduces trivial anxieties and encourages living meaningfully, focusing on values and relationships over petty concerns.

Inner Child Dialogue

Origin: Analytical Psychology (Carl Jung, modern trauma therapy)**Description:** Nurture and listen to the younger parts of yourself.**Real-world Use:** When you're upset or behaving in a way you don't quite understand, take a quiet moment to imagine your younger self at the age those feelings might have started. In your mind's eye, have a conversation: Ask that inner child what they're feeling and why. Let them speak. Then, as your adult self, comfort and reassure them: "I'm here for you. I won't abandon you. It's okay to feel this."

Shadow Integration

Origin: Analytical Psychology (Carl Jung)**Description:** Acknowledge and integrate the "dark" parts of yourself you normally reject.**Real-world Use:** Identify a trait in others that really irritates you – this could hint at your shadow. Write a dialogue or story where you let your shadow speak. Let that voice rant on paper. Then, reflect: What does it really want? Is there a valid message there? By acknowledging the shadow, you rob it of the power to trip you up. It becomes an integrated part of you, often turning into a strength.

Unconditional Self-Acceptance

Origin: Humanistic Psychology (Carl Rogers)**Description:** Approve of yourself as a whole, not because you're perfect, but because you're inherently worthy.**Real-world Use:** Develop a daily self-acceptance ritual. For instance, every morning look in the mirror and say, "I accept you fully, with strengths and flaws. You are enough." In the evening, note if you caught yourself in self-criticism – gently counter it: "Yes, I didn't do X well, but that doesn't make me a bad person. I still accept myself and can try again."

Life Audit & Future Self

Origin: Existential/Humanistic Psychology**Description:** Examine your life holistically and define who you want to become.**Real-world Use:** Take an afternoon with pen and paper. Draw columns for key areas of life (career, relationships, health, spirituality). Under each, write current state and ideal vision. Now imagine 5-10 years from now, your Future Self who has achieved many of those ideals. Write a letter from your future self to your present self, describing how life is different and what steps got you there.

Character Strengths Inventory

Origin: Positive Psychology (VIA Character Survey)**Description:** Discover and leverage your top strengths to express your true self.**Real-world Use:** Use a free resource like the VIA Character Strengths survey to identify your top 5 character strengths, or simply reflect on what you and others see as your strong suits. Once identified, ask: "Am

I using these strengths daily?" When you use signature strengths, you often feel more authentically "you" and more fulfilled.

Authenticity Check-ins

Origin: Existential Psychology (Sartre, Maslow)**Description:** Regularly ask if your actions match your true preferences and beliefs.**Real-world Use:** Set a weekly reminder with a simple question: "Is there anything I'm doing just to please others or out of habit, that doesn't feel true to me?" Also do positive check-ins: "When did I feel most myself this week? How can I create more of that?" Authenticity is deeply tied to purpose and identity; the more your outer life reflects your inner values and interests, the more meaningful life feels.

Legacy Project

Origin: Existential Psychology (Erik Erikson's generativity)**Description:** Do something that makes you feel you'll leave a positive mark – it solidifies a sense of identity as someone who contributes.**Real-world Use:** Think of a small legacy project: something you'd be proud to have as part of your story. It could be mentoring a younger person, writing a short book of lessons learned, creating a piece of art for your family, planting a community garden, or recording family history interviews. Dedicate some time each week to it.

High-Level Self-Definition

Origin: Narrative Therapy**Description:** Choose a concise definition for yourself that is positive and aspirational, and remind yourself of it often.**Real-world Use:** Write an "I am" statement that captures your best self or the self you strive to be, e.g., "I am a resilient, compassionate, and creative person who brings light to others." Memorize it. In the morning, recite it. When facing doubts or social pressure, recall it: "How would that version of me handle this?" This becomes a touchstone.

Discipline & Habits Tools

These techniques help you build consistent habits, overcome procrastination, and maintain self-discipline. Use them when starting new routines, breaking bad habits, or needing to stay motivated toward your goals.

Habit Stacking

Origin: Behavioral Psychology (BJ Fogg/James Clear)**Description:** Attach a new habit to an existing routine to build discipline easily.**Real-world Use:** If you want to start meditating (new habit), tie it to something you already do without fail, like morning coffee. E.g., "After I brew my morning coffee, I will sit and meditate for 2 minutes." The existing routine acts as a trigger. By piggybacking on a stable habit, the new behavior finds a stable slot in your day.

The Two-Day Rule

Origin: Productivity (Matt D'Avella)**Description:** Never skip a positive habit two days in a row.**Real-world Use:** You're aiming to write in your journal daily, but you missed Wednesday. According to the two-day rule, you make sure to write on Thursday. This way, an off day doesn't derail your progress. It's forgiving (acknowledges we're human and will slip) but also firm in preventing a lapse from becoming a relapse.

Visual Cues & Environment Design

Origin: Behavioral Design (James Clear's Atomic Habits)**Description:** Shape your surroundings to make good behaviors easy and bad ones hard.**Real-world Use:** Want to practice guitar daily? Leave the guitar on a stand in the middle of your living space. Want to be less hooked to your phone at work? Keep it in a drawer or another room. Trying to read more? Put a book on your pillow. By engineering default choices, you require less brute-force discipline.

Public Accountability

Origin: Behavioral Psychology**Description:** Commit your goal or habit to someone else or a group.**Real-world Use:** If you want to run three times a week, tell a friend your plan and schedule a quick check-in text each Sunday, or join a running club. By externalizing your commitment, you create a social contract: breaking it now has a cost (even if just mild embarrassment or letting someone down). For many, that's a stronger motivator than promises to oneself.

The 5-Second Rule

Origin: Motivational Psychology (Mel Robbins)**Description:** Count down 5-4-3-2-1 and move – don't give your brain time to make excuses.**Real-world Use:** Alarm goes off in the morning and you want to snooze? Instead, silently count 5-4-3-2-1 and on 1, swing your legs out of bed and stand up. Need to start an unpleasant task? 5-4-3-2-1, and begin typing or cleaning. The idea is to interrupt the mind's avoidance reflex by acting before it kicks in.

Temptation Bundling

Origin: Behavioral Psychology (Katherine Milkman)**Description:** Pair something you need discipline for with something you enjoy to make it more attractive.**Real-w

orld Use: Only allow yourself to watch your favorite Netflix show when you're at the gym (watch on the treadmill). Or, only listen to that juicy true-crime podcast while doing house cleaning. By bundling the "want" (entertainment) with the "should" (exercise/chores), you become eager to do the should because the want is attached.

Time Blocking & Protected Time

Origin: Productivity (Cal Newport)**Description:** Schedule dedicated blocks for your important tasks or habits and treat them as appointments.**Real-world Use:** If you decide that writing, exercise, or learning is important, block 7-8am (or any feasible time) on your calendar for it every weekday. During that block, nothing else is allowed to intrude. If someone asks for that time, it's already "booked." This enforces discipline by removing decision fatigue.

90-Second Rule for Cravings/Urges

Origin: Neuroscience-based**Description:** When you get a craving or urge that might break discipline, wait 90 seconds before acting – most urges significantly decrease by then.**Real-world Use:** You're working and suddenly crave a cookie or to scroll social media. Instead of immediately giving in, note the time, and say "I'll decide in 90 seconds." Use that time to do something else – take deep breaths, sip water, continue a bit of work, or just observe the urge. Often, by the end of 90 seconds, the intense pull has diminished.

Personal KPI or Streak Tracking

Origin: Productivity (Seinfeld's "Don't break the chain")**Description:** Track your consistency visibly and aim to keep a streak going.**Real-world Use:** Use a wall calendar, habit-tracking app, or journal. Each day you complete your target behavior, mark an X or color in that day. As days accumulate, you get a chain. The game becomes not breaking the chain. If you miss a day, start a new chain and see if you can beat your previous record.

Implementation Intentions

Origin: Social Psychology (Peter Gollwitzer)**Description:** Forming a concrete plan that links a specific situation with a planned action: "If X happens, then I will do Y."**Real-world Use:** To build a reading habit, set an intention: "If it's 9 pm and I'm free, then I'll read for 20 minutes before bed." By deciding this in advance, when 9 pm arrives and you're tempted to scroll on your phone, the mental plan kicks in and steers you to pick up a book instead.

Pomodoro Technique

Origin: Time Management (Francesco Cirillo)**Description:** Working in focused bursts (commonly 25 minutes) followed by short breaks to enhance concentration and prevent burnout.**Real-world Use:** When you have a daunting study session or work project, set a timer for 25 minutes and give the task your full attention. When time's up, take a 5-minute break to stretch or rest. Repeat this cycle. Knowing a break is always coming makes it easier to start and maintain focus.

Eat the Frog

Origin: Proverbial Wisdom (Mark Twain, popularized by Brian Tracy)**Description:** Doing the most unpleasant or important task first thing in the day, so you get it done and relieve anxiety about it.**Real-world Use:** If you dread doing your taxes, plan to tackle it first thing Saturday morning. Once that's out of the way, you'll feel a surge of relief and accomplishment. The rest of the day will feel easier in comparison, and you won't have the tax task looming over you anymore.

Quick Reference Guide

When you need help with:

Intense emotions: Try Dichotomy of Control, Emotion Labeling, 4-7-8 Breathing, Objective Description

Decision paralysis: Try Pre-Mortem Analysis, Cost of Inaction, 10-10-10 Rule, Third-Person Self-Talk

Anxiety & panic: Try Box Breathing, 5-4-3-2-1 Grounding, Progressive Muscle Relaxation, Thought Labeling

Feeling down or hopeless: Try Behavioral Activation, Mastery Experiences, Physical Exercise, Finding Your Why

Bouncing back from setbacks: Try Obstacle → Opportunity, Gratitude in Adversity, Incremental Improvement, Active Problem-Solving

Finding meaning & purpose: Try Ikigai, Values Clarification, Legacy Project, Find Your "Why"

Building consistent habits: Try Habit Stacking, Two-Day Rule, Environment Design, Temptation Bundling

Remember to practice these techniques regularly – like any skill, they improve with use. Start with 1-2 tools that resonate with your current situation, master them, and then gradually expand your toolkit.

Afterword

CONTINUE YOUR JOURNEY

Thank you for joining me on this exploration of personal development through "The Warrior and the Sage: Endless Journey." The principles and practices in this book are just the beginning of what's possible when you commit to authentic growth.

Ready to take your transformation deeper?

Visit **treydoravr.com** to discover our comprehensive online courses, including an expanded, interactive version of the journey you've begun in this book.

On the website, you'll find:

-

- Video tutorials expanding on key   concepts

-

- Downloadable worksheets and   exercises

-

- Community support from fellow   travelers

-

- Advanced practices for continued   growth

-

- Personal coaching opportunities

Your journey doesn't end with the last page of this book—it continues with each choice you make, each practice you implement, and each insight you integrate.

I look forward to supporting your continued growth.

With gratitude,

Mark Loudermilk

ABOUT THE AUTHOR

"I discovered that my life's story wasn't written in permanent ink,but in pencil—waiting for me to erase the lines that no longer served me and redraw my own path forward."

My transformation began between the confined walls of a prison library,where books became portals to worlds beyond my physical limitations. What began as an escape from my reality evolved into the very key that would unlock my future. The ancient wisdom of the Stoics taught me that while I couldn't control my circumstances, I held absolute dominion over my response to them.

"In those quiet moments surrounded by dog-eared pages, I realized that true freedom isn't granted by unlocked doors, but by an unlocked mind."

The philosophers and leaders whose words filled those pages became my unseen mentors, teaching me to view my challenges not as life sentences but as temporary chapters in a much longer story. Their centuries-old wisdom provided a framework for understanding my modern struggles—revealing that anxiety often stems from grasping at what lies beyond our control, while peace comes from focusing on what lies within it.

When physical freedom finally came, I approached education not as a requirement but as a revolution. Each degree I pursued—respiratory therapy,nursing, and later computer science—wasn't merely a credential but a declaration that my past would not dictate my future.

"The hospital corridors where I worked for over twenty years became my second classroom, where I learned that healing others was, in many ways,healing myself."

Emergency rooms and intensive care units taught me lessons no text book could convey: that life is fragile yet remarkably resilient; that courage wears many faces; that sometimes the most profound act of strength is simply showing up day after day. In witnessing countless human stories unfold—some ending in triumph, others in heartbreak—I gained perspective that transformed my understanding of what truly matters.

"The distance between who I was and who I became wasn't measured in years or achievements, but in the gradual expansion of what I believed possible for myself."

My path eventually led to entrepreneurship, where I discovered that building businesses shared something essential with rebuilding a life: both require vision to see what doesn't yet exist, courage to move forward despite uncertainty, and persistence to transform setbacks into stepping stones.

"The same mind that once plotted escape routes from dead-end streets now designs pathways for others to find their own freedom."

Today, my deepest conviction is that transformation is not a privilege reserved for the few but a birthright available to anyone willing to challenge their own limitations. The journey from incarcerated youth to healthcare professional to entrepreneur stands not as a testimony to my uniqueness, but to the universal human capacity for reinvention.

This book distills the wisdom that guided my metamorphosis—practical tools forged in the crucible of real struggle and tested against the unforgiving anvil of life. These aren't abstract theories but battle-tested strategies that carried me from darkness into light.

"If these pages contain any wisdom, it's this: your greatest limitations in life aren't the walls around you, but the walls you build within you."

I offer these insights not from a pedestal of perfection, but from the trenches of transformation—as someone who has stumbled, fallen, and risen again. My hope is that something within these chapters resonates with your own journey, sparking the recognition that change is not only possible but inevitable when you decide to pick up the pen and rewrite your story.

Connect with me and continue your journey of personal development at treydoravr. com,where the principles in this book come alive through interactive courses designed to guide your own transformation.

www.ingramcontent.com/pod-product-compliance
Lightning Source LLC
Chambersburg PA
CBHW051522120626
46551CB00012B/1043